Thanks

There are many people whc   ice to
me as I gathered material fo. ....

To Maria Laura Volante who welcomed me to Picinisco so many
years ago and has continued to be a wonderful friend. Maria Laura
was my first interpreter in Picinisco, as she speaks French, English
and Italian. She drove me to San Gennaro and helped me find my
great great grandfather's grave there. And she spent hours
answering every question I had about what it was like growing up in
Picinisco. She also opened her home to me and my family and
cooks like a Michelin chef!

To Michele Vacca who generously gives his time to maintain a very
comprehensive website about Picinisco (www.picinisco.net) and
provides access to Picinisco's historic church records to people all
over the world who have ancestors from Picinisco. When Michele
and I first met many years ago, he spoke only French and I only
English, but we managed to communicate with one another and
become good friends. Michele introduced me to many lovely
people in Picinisco, drove me around to all the places I had only
ever read about, and shared many meals with me in Picinisco.

To Daniele Venditti, the concierge at Sotto le Stelle in Picinisco, for
always making me feel so welcome in Picinisco. To say that
Daniele goes above and beyond what one would expect from a
concierge is an understatement of grand proportion. Daniele made
it his business to know who I was and what I wanted from my visit to
Picinisco and then did everything in his power to fulfill even the
wishes I didn't know I had!

The Pacitti family who operate Casa Lawrence have been so
welcoming to me and my family on every occasion that I have
visited. They have shared fabulous meals with me at their
restaurant and beautiful spreads of cheese, wine and pastries in
their backyard, they gave me an apron and let me join them in
making ricotta and pecorino cheese, and offered encouragement
and support for my book.

At the library in Atina (Biblioteca del Comune di Atina), Luciano
Caira, the archivist, very kindly showed me many books and
photographs of Picinisco I never could have found on my own.
Luciano suffered my rudimentary Italian, gave me great advice on

where to get lunch in Atina, and introduced me to all the historians who were working in the library while I visited.

To Cesidio di Ciacca whose enthusiasm for Picinisco is infectious. I had heard about all the work Cesidio was doing in Picinisco for years before I actually met him. Suddenly there he was in the piazza one evening: we met, fell to talking, and didn't stop for hours. When I told him I intended to write this book he sent me articles and photographs and waded through my earliest manuscript with care and attention. His comments were insightful, inspiring and invaluable.

And to my family and friends, who visited Picinisco with me, willingly listened to all my tidbits of Picinisco history, commiserated with me during the challenges of writing, rewriting and publishing, read and edited my manuscript, and otherwise offered endless support and enthusiasm, I thank you too!

PICINISCO

UNCOVERING 1000 YEARS OF HISTORY

Virginia Arcari

Virginia Arcari
arcari.picinisco1000@gmail.com

Book Layout © 2016 BookDesignTemplates.com

Picinisco: Uncovering 1000 Years of History/Virginia Arcari. -- 1st ed.
ISBN 978-0-692-84193-8

Forward

The first time I heard the name "Picinisco" was over twenty years ago when I began a family genealogy project. My father, the only one of his family to emigrate from Glasgow, Scotland to the United States, certainly knew his family was originally from Italy. But he was no help with trying to find out where in Italy our family had come from. I had better luck with my aunt who lived in Glasgow; she told me the Arcari family was from a place called "San Gennaro". Helpful, but confusing since there are so many places in Italy with that name. But one day, somewhere among the birth certificates, burial records and photos spread across her kitchen table, my aunt and I found the name Picinisco and connected it to the hamlet of San Gennaro. I had finally I found a place in Italy to begin my research.

I started searching at the Mormon Family History Center in New York City, where I live. They had census records from Picinisco from the 1800s and I was able to find my Arcari family among them. Once I was certain where my family came from, I was desperate to visit. I was celebrating my birthday during a family vacation in Rome when my husband surprised me with a day trip to Picinisco. We got lost trying to get there, of course! But when we finally drove up the mountain and into the piazza and I got out and looked at the expansive view of the gorgeous Comino Valley, literally at my feet, I fell in love with the place. From that point on I wanted to know everything about Picinisco.

There was one small problem: I couldn't find any materials to aid in my research. While I was in the town of Picinisco I bought every book I could find at the little tourist office, but the books were all in Italian and I couldn't read a word of it. (Out of frustration I began to study Italian thinking someday I could actually read some of the books I bought in Picinisco - a very slow route to the information I sought!). I scoured the New York Public Library but couldn't find any historical information under the subject heading of "Picinisco". Twenty years ago, the Internet had very little information about the town of Picinisco, apart from some simple tourism sites. However, the genealogy community that was just getting started on the internet did yield results for me. I was very lucky to find two people who were also fascinated with the Arcaris of Picinisco: John Gerrard and Anita Arcari Pugh. John was an amateur genealogist from Scotland who moved to Arizona. (After World War II John's father dropped his last name of Arcari and used his middle name, Gerrard, instead). We began corresponding and exchanging information about our families - convinced that we were somehow related to one another. What John knew about Picinisco came from a book he had managed to find that was written by Vincenzo Arcari in the 1950s; it was called "La Storia di Picinisco." The book was in Italian and John had painstakingly translated much of it into English with the use of a very early computer translation software program. I will never forget his generosity in sharing his translation with me; for the first time I had research material I could dig into.

A short time after John and I connected with one another, I found Anita Arcari Pugh. Anita's Arcari family left Picinisco for England and settled there establishing an ice cream business, just as my family had in Glasgow. We shared photographs and family trees and I introduced her online to John Gerrard and together we all found our connection to one another - going back some six generations! I also read the first article Anita wrote about the "hokey pokey man" (Italians who sold ice cream on the streets of cities in Great Britain), and later her book of the same name, a great story full of helpful information about the life of a Piciniscani immigrant.

As my understanding of the region grew I was able to find more information on the history of Picinisco, but only at a very basic level. Italian language treatises that I was finally (almost) able to read were not addressing the questions I really wanted to answer: what did the people of Picinisco do every day, how did they dress, what did they eat? I went ahead and published my Arcari family history about ten years later and included all the historical references I had been able to find. Although there was not nearly enough history in the book for me, I was surprised to discover that some of my Scottish acquaintances, whose own families came from Picinisco, were interested in reading my genealogy book. They visited Picinisco regularly, some even from the time they were children, but they knew very little about the history of the town and really wanted to know more.

So, I set out to write this history of Picinisco, partially for the people who love the town but who do not speak Italian, but mostly to satisfy my desire to know more about the people I came from. I've done my best to find scholarly sources for all of the material, but have chosen not to add footnotes because almost every reference would be to an Italian text. The book is organized into chapters dealing with various topics that have most interested me. It begins with an examination of the settlement of the town 1,000 years ago and its history under feudal ownership and eventually as an independent "comune" in the Province of Frosinone. With that historical backdrop, the rest of the book deals with the questions that have been more challenging to research: for example, marriage and the relationship between the sexes in Picinisco; the life of shepherds in the mountains around Picinisco; why the Piciniscani became famous for modeling; the role of religion in their daily lives, and so on. As a person born and raised in the United States, I am aware that my own cultural bias may have had an influence on the presentation of the material in these pages, and apologize for any missteps. I also acknowledge that there are likely errors that will need correction, and invite any and all constructive criticism. For me, it has been a labor of love.

Introduction

The first written evidence of the mountaintop town of Picinisco dates the town's origins to at least 1017AD, 1000 years ago. The people who settled there were looking for a safe place to live where they could grow enough food to feed their families and follow the teachings of Catholicism. They lived simple, fairly isolated lives on top of the mountain, relying on their own ingenuity to survive. While foreign powers controlled southern Italy from the capital in Naples for hundreds of years, the Piciniscani followed the dictates of whatever feudal lord controlled the various towns in the Comino Valley.

What set Picinisco apart from other small agro-pastoral towns in southern Italy, then and now, is the glorious natural beauty and bounty of its position. The town is surrounded by fertile hillside pastures filled with wild herbs, vegetables and berries, forests with every variety of tree, clean and roaring rivers rushing from snow-covered mountaintops, wild animals in abundance, and a vista of the entire valley of Comino at its feet. It was also uniquely situated as a center for the exchange of commerce between the shepherds of the summer mountain pastures and the farmers of the lower hilly region. In its economic heyday, during the 1700s and 1800s, Picinisco and its surrounding communities had almost 4000 people living and working in the area. The town was bustling with activity, with numerous shops, craftsmen, and prosperous businesses like a dairy, paper mill, olive press, mining and textile manufacturing.

Like many small towns in southern Italy, Picinisco's economy began to decline at the end of the 1800s. When Italy became a single state in 1861 the new national government promised improved economic opportunities for the south of Italy, but they never materialized. Instead, a violent and bloody fight ensued as the north and south battled over the changing political situation. Many southern Italians chose to abandon their homes after Italian unification and the Piciniscani were among them. The decline in population, damage from earthquakes, and bombings during World War II caused even more economic decline over the next few decades. By the 1960s there were only 1200 people left in Picinisco, the same number that exists today.

With considerable effort on the part of its residents and descendants of Piciniscani natives, the town has reemerged as a center of tourism for the Comino Valley. The town's charming historic character is completely preserved. New restaurants and hotels are available and access to the National Park makes Picinisco an attractive location for exploring the Comino Valley. There are many festivals of historic, culinary and literary celebration that take place in Picinisco today. Worldwide recognition has been given to the pecorino cheese of Picinisco and many other local foods and wine. The town is reemerging as a cultural center in the Comino Valley.

CONTENTS

Chapter 1

Place Names

The country of Italy is today divided into twenty different "regions" and the town of Picinisco is located in the region called Lazio. Lazio is in the south of Italy and its largest city is Rome. The region of Lazio is divided into five "provinces" and Picinisco is found in the province of Frosinone. Frosinone lies on the southeastern edge of Lazio, sharing a border with the Italian regions of Molise and Abruzzo. The National Park of Abruzzo, Lazio and Molise, the oldest and certainly one of the largest parks in Italy today, has one of its main entrances in Picinisco. The Park and the town are located in the mountain range called Monti della Meta – the largest peak being Monte Meta (formerly known as Monte Acze) with an elevation in excess of 2200 meters, located just behind Picinisco. The lower heights of the Monti della Meta region are called the Mainarde Range. Two rivers dominate the landscape: the Melfa which runs from the base of Mount Meta, and the Mollarino which begins near the Picinisco hamlet of San Gennaro, both of which flow into the River Liri.

The town of Picinisco sits at an elevation of 725 meters above sea level. The "comune" (township) of Picinisco includes 62 kilometers (24 square miles) of land. Most of the land is high mountain pastures and rich forests, with farms and vineyards at the lower elevations and smaller hamlets dotting the landscape.

Historical material dealing specifically with Picinisco is very limited as it is a relatively small town. However, it is possible to gain some insight from historical sources dealing with slightly broader geographic areas that include the town of Picinisco. These areas have been variously identified over the years and the following place names are useful in any historical research.

Terra di San Benedetto. The Terra di San Benedetto refers to an area of land (including Picinisco) transferred to the Abbey of Montecassino in 744AD. This is one of the oldest place-name references to the countryside that includes Picinisco.

Val di Comino. Picinisco is located in the valley of Comino, and this geographical reference has been in use since early Roman times. The name "Comino" is taken from "Cominium," the name of a city destroyed in 293BC during one of the Samnite wars. The Valley is a little over 25 miles long running northwest to southeast along the mountains' edge. In general, the Val di Comino includes both the flat lands of the physical valley and the small mountaintop towns perched on either side of the valley. The townships that are part of the Val di Comino include: Alvito, Atina, Belmont Castello, Broccostella, Campoli Appennino, Casalattico, Casalvieri, Fontechiari, Gallinaro, Pescosolido, Picinisco, Posta Fibreno, San Biagio Saracinisco, San Donato, Settefrati, Terelle, Vicalvi, and Villa Latina.

Duchy of Alvito. Beginning in the 1400s, a feudal estate that included ten towns in the Comino Valley became known as the Duchy of Alvito. The town of Alvito (within the Duchy) was a kind of "capital" of the Duchy. The other towns of the Duchy included: Atina, Belmonte Castello, Campoli Appennino, Gallinaro, Picinisco, Posta Fibreno, San Donato, Settefrati, and Vicalvi.

Terra di Lavoro. The term "Terra di Lavoro" (land of labor) was the medieval name of a province in southern Italy within the Kingdom of Naples. This province included portions of what is now southern Lazio, northern Campania and northwest Molise. Within Terra di Lavoro there were many political districts, including the district (often also called a "province" itself) of Caserta. Picinisco was within this district of Caserta, in the province of Terra di Lavoro. Terra di Lavoro existed as a separate province until 1927, when it was broken apart into smaller provinces, including a new province called Frosinone. Picinisco is now in the province of Frosinone.

Ciociaria. The term "Ciociaria" is used to refer to a group of people from southern Italy who shared the same rural living conditions and traditions and spoke a similar dialect called "ciociaro". The geographic area of the Ciociaria roughly equates to what is now the province of Frosinone. The name itself derives from the traditional footwear worn by the peasants of this region called "ciocie" (flat sandals with leather straps that lace up the leg). The Piciniscani are included among those identified as ciociaria.

Mezzogiorno. The term "Mezzogiorno" was adopted as a reference to southern Italy (particularly, the Kingdoms of Naples and Sicily). When Italy was unified as a single country in 1861, the people of southern Italy were stereotyped as a backward, uneducated group, principally because of the differences in their economy (the south being viewed as primarily rural and the north more industrial) and in their socialization (southerners being viewed as very poor, primitive people compared to the northerners who identified themselves with the advancements of the larger industrialized European community). This stereotype continues to be used today as part of a largely uninformed and insupportable assumption that southern Italians are inferior to northern Italians. Recently historians have focused on this so-called "southern question" and begun to dispute the basis of these assumptions. The modern view is that before Italian unification, the south was a wealthy, sophisticated, innovative and prosperous part of Italy that was largely destroyed in the process of unification by an oppressive national government.

Chapter 2

Milestones in Progression from Early Settlement to Comune

The Comino Valley, where Picinisco is located, has been inhabited since early Roman times. It is mentioned in Livy's History of Rome, as the place where the Romans clashed with the Samnites in 293BC, and in Virgil's Aeneid. Early Roman coins and tombs discovered in Picinisco also support the presence of an early settlement there. The Comino Valley was important to the Romans because of the discovery of iron and copper deposits on Mt. Meta that were essential to the production of weaponry and military armor as well as tools. Some historians speculate that the first settlement at Picinisco may have been part of an early mountaintop lookout system established in the Comino Valley to protect these mining operations.

The first actual written record of a specific settlement in the area that now comprises the comune of Picinisco appears in a document dated 894AD, referring to a monastery called "San Valentino". That document suggests that the San Valentino monastery was established by the Abbey of Montecassino, which became the owner of the land from a contribution it received in 744AD. This history of Picinisco begins with that 744AD transfer.

Land Grant of 744AD. The first document referring to land in the Comino Valley that definitely included what is today the comune of Picinisco was recorded in 744AD, when Duke Gisulfo II of Benevento granted control of the area to the Montecassino Abbey. Because of this land donation, the Abbey became the capital of a "state" known as the "Terra di San Benedetto," the secular lands belonging to and under the control of the Abbey.

The Montecassino Abbey was a Benedictine abbey that functioned autonomously, accountable only to the Pope, which was unusual for an abbey in this time period. As such, it was an important political force among the city-states of the coastal region (Naples, Gaeta and Amalfi). Strategically, the Abbey was a fortress located on top of a large mountain overlooking the town of Cassino (then called "San Germano") at the southern entrance to the Comino Valley. Because the Montecassino Abbey had political autonomy and a strategically defensible position, wealthy nobles were eager to make land grants to the Abbey to secure its support. The 744AD land grant helped Duke Gisulfo II secure the border of his Benevento Duchy against the coastal city-states.

Sometime after this 744AD land grant, the Montecassino Abbey established the monastery of San Valentino in what would later become the comune of Picinisco. (San Valentino was located below the town of Picinisco, in a hamlet now called Immoglie). According to the "Benedictine Way," land under the control of the Abbey was organized and operated so as to be productive and provide economic support to the Abbey. Small farms were established around a church and/or monastery by servants and small farmers and a manorial economy developed to support the population and the monks and priests of the church. These small communities attracted craftsmen who produced tools necessary for a manorial economy (typically made of wood or iron) and often local markets for exchange and barter would follow. The population lived fairly peacefully and had no real defensive needs.

The Terra di San Benedetto stayed in the hands of the Montecassino Abbey for the next century. In 866AD, Louis II (Roman Emperor and King of Italy) transferred it to another Benedictine abbey - the Abbey of San Vincenzo al Volturno. The Volturno Abbey was located some 50 kilometers north and east of the Montecassino Abbey. This land parcel that included Picinisco then became part of the "Terra di San Vincenzo". The Abbey at San Vincenzo al Volturno was, like Montecassino, a powerful landowner thanks to donations from the Benevento nobles. Louis II had been having trouble with the disruptive Duchy of Capua, a strong ally of the Montecassino Abbey, and his rationale for transferring the land away from Montecassino to San Vincenzo al Volturno may have been to weaken the Montecassino Abbey's alliance with Capua.

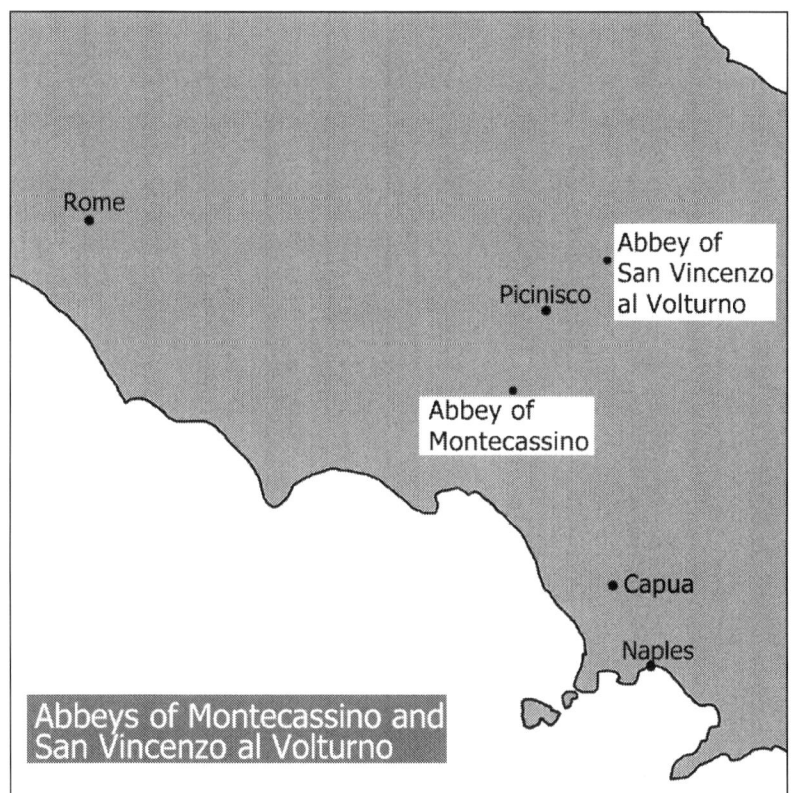

Abbeys of Montecassino and San Vincenzo al Volturno

Saracen Invasion. During the period from 881 through 888, the Saracens invaded the Comino Valley and ransacked the Abbeys of Montecassino and San Vincenzo al Volturno. Saracens were Muslims from Arabia who used their powerful navies to raid the weaker European-Christian Mediterranean coastlines during the Middle Ages, seeking slaves and goods. The monks of both Montecassino and San Vincenzo al Volturno were forced to flee to Capua for the next few decades. With these powerful Abbeys gone, members of the local nobility (principally, the Marsi and Aquino families described below) were able to step in and gain control over various parcels of the Abbeys' landholdings.

Incastellamento. Following the Saracen massacre in the Comino Valley, there was an understandable fear of invasion and a desire to provide a more defensive position for the property of the nobility and the Abbeys. Also, the local population had been wiped out during the invasion and repopulation was imperative to make the land productive. These needs gave rise to a period of history in southern Italy known as the period of "incastellamento." This was a time of purposeful land development designed to achieve three objectives: the formation of new settlements for more effective land development and management; the fortification of the settlements for defensive purposes, to protect against future invasion; and the empowerment of the settlements with self-jurisdiction so they could operate effectively without having to wait for direction from a faraway landowner.   Although the term "incastellamento" implies this new plan for land development included a castle, that was not the case.   The plan called for towns with walls or towers or a fortification that would improve their defensive positions.   This reform scheme allowed the local nobility (and eventually the returning Abbeys) to attract new families to settle areas that could be protected and governed more efficiently.   Incastellamento began in the flatter valley of Comino and soon expanded with the creation of many of the mountaintop towns like Picinisco (nearby Settefrati and Alvito, for example, were founded during this same period).

The process of incastellamento helped revive the earliest Picinisco settlement of San Valentino. In a document, dated in 894AD, the abbot of San Vincenzo al Volturno (Maione) granted permission to two brothers (Grifone and Leone, sons of Teobaldo from the nearby town of Atina) to use the San Valentino settlement for their own gain, until the death of the third generation of their male descendants.   This concession document confirmed that the San Valentino monastery had been destroyed (likely during the Saracen invasion).   Since the monks of San Vincenzo al Volturno would not return to their abbey until 914AD, this concession ensured the land would be protected and redeveloped in their absence.

During the next 100 years, it is unclear which of the Abbeys controlled the San Valentino settlement. The brothers Grifone and Leone owed their allegiance to San Vincenzo al Volturno, but in a 944AD declaration by the Pope describing all the land that was part of the San Vincenzo al Volturno holdings, the area of San Valentino was not specifically included.   The monks from Montecassino returned to their Abbey in 950AD and began a concerted effort to recapture their earlier landholdings.   The settlement at San Valentino was mentioned again in documents in 960AD and 981AD – not specifically identifying it as part of Montecassino or San Vincenzo al Volturno – but providing confirmation of its existence at the end of the tenth century.   The Abbey at San Vincenzo al

Volturno was never able to fully regain its position as a powerful landowner after the Saracen invasion. This vacuum created an opportunity for land acquisition by local nobles.

First Written Reference to "Picinisco" - 1017AD. In a document dated March 6, 1017, the Picinisco settlement of San Valentino (lying within the principality of Capua) was transferred by the Princes of Capua (Pandolfo III and IV) back to the Montecassino Abbey. The document states that San Valentino had been attacked and lay in ruin for some years before this 1017AD transfer. The Princes of Capua had been informed by their brother, the abbot of Montecassino, that recently "Ponzo, son of Allone," had rebuilt the San Valentino church and village. By this transfer, Montecassino acquired the San Valentino church, the surrounding village and farmland, and the right to build a mill on the river. The importance of the document is that it contains the first specific written reference to "Picinisco" (actually spelled "Piczinisci" in the document) as the name of the place where San Valentino was located. Before this time, the San Valentino settlement was always indentified as a kind of neighborhood of the nearby city of Atina.

Picinisco - Origins of the Name. There has been some controversy among historians about the origin of the name of the town of Picinisco. (Besides the original spelling "Piczinisci," the town's name has been recorded as "Piceno" and "Picenisco"). Some early historians argued that the name was that of a famous Saracen general, while others argued that it originated with the Latin "Pica" (a bird) or "Pico or "Picco" (the name of a cypress tree in the nearby mountains). Recently, historians suggest that the more likely explanation is that, following the Saracen invasion, some invaders decided to settle in the area and paid tribute to their Saracen origins with their choice of name. (Note that nearby San Biagio di Saracinisco has a similar name that might have the same origin).

First Written Reference to Mountaintop Town of Picinisco - 1054AD. The first specific written description of the mountaintop town of Picinisco (as opposed to the San Valentino settlement in the valley) appears in a historical document dated in 1054AD. The document actually dealt with a donation of land located in nearby San Biagio di Saracinisco to the Montecassino Abbey by the brothers Oderisio II and Rinaldo III of the Marsi family. But, in this document, there is a statement that the Marsi brothers were residing in the mountaintop village of Picinisco.

According to the document Picinisco was at this time an established settlement with a strong tower and a circular wall that included gates that could be locked to protect inhabitants. The document was drawn up by a judge and notary of Picinisco and witnessed by inhabitants of the town indicating that, by 1054AD, Picinisco already had some structure and regulation guiding the behavior of its citizens.

Local Nobles. The mountaintop town of Picinisco and surrounding area was, at various times from the eleventh century through the end of the fifteenth century, controlled by the Marsi, Aquino and Cantelmo families, all important members of the nobility of southern Italy. Early on in this period, as a "neighborhood" of the nearby town of Atina, Picinisco was governed by the noble family in control there. By the end of the fourteenth century, all of the towns of the Comino Valley (including Picinisco) were consolidated as a single estate under the control of the "Count" of Alvito; a century later, the estate became known as the "Duchy of Alvito."

It is difficult to be certain which particular member of these families had control or influence over Picinisco at any given time because ownership was often shared among several members of the same family (sometimes with each receiving only a percentage ownership of a particular town) and ownership shifted as a result of marriage or inheritance. Also, many members of these families shared the same first names which makes tracing their existence from generation to generation very difficult. We do know that the family members typically managed their interests jointly in order to maintain a strong position (defensively and economically) permitting us to examine their influence with reference to particular time periods.

Marsi Family. The Conti dei Marsi mentioned in the 1054AD document described above were originally from the southern part of the Duchy of Spoleto. The family was large and its holdings were vast during the 10th and 11th centuries. Many members of the family were monks and even abbots at the Abbeys of Montecassino and San Vincenzo al Volturno; others were put into positions of religious authority when the family captured new territory and established their own monasteries. In 1087, Oderisio Marsi was elected the 39th Abbot of Montecassino. He was the son of

Oderisio II, one of the Marsi brothers who made the 1054AD land grant described above.

When the great Abbeys abandoned the Comino Valley after the Saracen invasion, the powerful Marsi lords took (likely by force) large tracts of land as their own and helped establish new fortified towns during the incastellamento period. When the Benedictines returned to Montecassino, the counts of Marsi made gifts of some of their now fortified towns back to the Abbey. The Marsi objective was to establish an alliance with Montecassino – primarily for defensive reasons – and the Abbey used the resources of families like the Marsi, who could bring new settlers from Spoleto and elsewhere to the region, to repopulate land in the spirit of incastellamento.

The particular branch of the Marsi family active in the vicinity of Picinisco was headed by Rainaldo di Marsi who is mentioned in various land documents in the late tenth century. His son Bernardo was the father of Oderisio II and Rinaldo III, the brothers who lived in the Picinisco castle at the time of the 1054AD donation to Montecassino. We have no evidence of how long the Marsi family exerted control over Picinisco, but we do know that eventually the family splintered into various factions and within a decade after the 1054AD donation, family squabbles diminished their ability to manage their holdings in the Comino Valley in a cohesive way.

Aquino Family. The Aquino family, the next noble family in control in the Comino Valley, descended from the Lombards, a Germanic people who conquered the north of Italy in the 6th Century and part of the south by the late 9th century. They became part of the nobility in the Duchies of Benevento and Capua. Early mention of the Aquino family near Montecassino is found in the 950s, when the Abbot Aligerno of Montecassino returned to the Abbey after the Saracen invasion and found himself challenged by Adenolfo Aquino, the Count of Aquino and Pontecorvo (located about 18 kilometers to the west of the Montecassino Abbey). The battles between the Aquinos and the Abbey continued (toward the end of the 900s) with then Abbot Manso as he attempted to further expand Montecassino's reach.

During the eleventh century, the Aquino family became allied with the Prince of Capua, Pandolfo IV, who frequently clashed with the Montecassino Abbey. As the Montecassino Abbey reacquired landholdings lost after the Saracen invasion, the Abbey began to reassert its political influence and Pandolfo IV of Capua found the Aquino family a helpful ally against the Abbey.   Two Aquino brothers, Adenolfo (the Duke of Gaeta and a Count of Aquino) and Landone, married the daughters of Prince Pandolfo IV of Capua. By the end of the eleventh century, the Aquino family extended its reach to the Comino Valley when Adenolfo (son of Landone) assumed the title of "Conte di Atina," which area then included Picinisco.   The title was inherited by his son Adenolfo at the beginning of the twelfth century.   However, with the Norman invasion this "Adenolfo" Aquino was forced to turn over his holdings to King Roger II.

Norman Invasion; Land Transfer of 1150AD; Early Feudal Estates. The Norman invasion of southern Italy took place over a period from the tenth to the eleventh centuries.   By 1130 Roger II was crowned King of Sicily (then including Sicily and what became the Kingdom of Naples) and embarked upon a mission to create a strong unitary state capable of defending its northern border.   The Normans favored a highly organized and well-administered government. To consolidate his control over large tracts of land and ensure loyalty to the crown, the king rewarded the nobles who had provided him with military support by making them "lords" of their own "feudal estate." The king granted the lord possession of a tract of land (and the income therefrom) and in exchange required him to raise an army to fight for the king and collect taxes for the crown as needed.

The first move toward establishing a feudal estate in Atina (that then included Picinisco) was made by Roger II in 1142AD when he appointed brothers Francesco Aquino (the Count of Laureto and Adriano) and Andrea Aquino (maestro of the army) to positions of authority in Atina.   Francesco essentially ruled economically and Andrea militarily, although the Montecassino Abbey continued to own property in Atina.   A few years later, in 1150AD, Roger II extinguished the Abbey's remaining landholdings in Atina and named Francesco and Andrea Aquino as feudal lords. The Aquino family continued in power for the next hundred years, although on several occasions the king punished the family by transferring ownership back to the Montecassino Abbey for a few years at a time.

The Aquino family controlled other property in the Comino Valley throughout the period following the Norman invasion: specifically, the towns of Alvito and Aquino and their surrounds. In 1248AD, when the king once again reaffirmed the Aquino family's ownership of Atina, all the family's landholdings in the Comino Valley were aggregated and referred to as a "baronia."

In 1260AD, Charles I of Anjou conquered the Kingdom of Naples and Sicily, which he and his offspring reigned through the end of the century and into the next. The Aquino family lost and gained landholdings in the Comino Valley with every change in Anjou leadership in the Kingdom. The baronia was broken apart and eventually the Aquinos lost their hold over Atina and Picinisco in 1312AD. King Robert of Anjou then gave the land to Giacomo di Capua, the son of an important government official. When Giacomo di Capua died, his daughter Giovanna inherited his interest in Atina. Giovanna di Capua was married to Giacomo Cantelmo who was part of the next family to become feudal landowners in the region. The Aquino family tried to maintain their holdings through various marriages with the Cantelmo family, but their influence continued to diminish through the 1300s.

Cantelmo Family. In 1269AD the Cantelmo family began acquiring feudal property in the Comino Valley, after siding with Charles I d'Anjou in the 1266AD battle for Naples. Their military support and political maneuvering brought them many estates in southern Italy. Giacomo Cantelmo became the feudal lord of Popoli and Alvito and maintained those holdings for generations. With his marriage to Giovanna di Capua, he added large parts of Atina to his holdings. Strategic marriages with the Aquino family brought more properties into the Cantelmo portfolio. Complete consolidation of control over the Comino Valley finally took place late in the fourteenth century when the remaining Aquino holdings in Atina and its surrounds became part of the dowry of Elisabetta d'Aquino, who married another Giacomo Cantelmo in 1386. Finally, in 1404, Giacomo Cantelmo was identified as the first "Count of Alvito" which then included the entire Comino Valley.

The Cantelmo family holdings were inherited by Giacomo's son Antonio Cantelmo (1406 – 1439) and then Antonio's son Nicolo Cantelmo (1440 - 1454). The next Count of Alvito, Pietro Giovanpaolo Cantelmo, had his title changed to that of a duke and the property then became known as the "Duchy of Alvito." This new Duke argued with King Ferdinand I of Naples and, by the 1470s, had lost much of his hold over the Duchy. His sons, Sigismondo and Ferrando, finally lost the entire feudal estate at the end of the 1400s to King Frederick of Naples.

Borgia & Navarro & Cardona. The next three families to control the Duchy of Alvito likely never stepped foot in the Comino Valley. They all appointed local governors to act on their behalf and happily collected income from the Duchy. The first of these was Gioffre Borgia, son of Pope Alexander VI and brother to Cesare, Giovanni and Lucrecia Borgia. As a young boy, he married the daughter of King Alfonso II of Naples in 1497 and received the Duchy as part of his wife's dowry. When his wife died in 1506, Gioffre had to forfeit the Duchy of Alvito to then King of Naples, Ferdinand II of Aragon.

Pietro Navarro was a Spanish military engineer and general. He became the next owner of the Alvito Duchy in 1507AD in recognition of his military service to the crown in Naples. When Navarro was captured by the French and began fighting with the army of Francis I of France against Milan in 1515AD, he too forfeited the Duchy.

The Cardona family was one of the great families of Aragon. In 1505AD, Ferdinand II of Aragon made Raimondo Cardona the Viceroy of Naples, and later Sicily, and eventually commander in chief of the Spanish forces in Italy. In 1515AD he was given title to the Duchy of Alvito. Like his predecessors, Cardona never lived in the Duchy and ruled through a local governor, enjoying the income of the property. He was not at all well-liked by the Piciniscani and many supported local "brigands" (groups of bandits) protesting Cardona's harsh treatment of his subjects. Following Raimondo Cardona's death in 1522AD, his son Ferrante de Cardona inherited the Duchy (1522AD - 1572AD) and passed it along to his sons, Loise (1572AD – 1574AD) and Antonio (1574AD – 1592AD).

Feudal properties were generally permitted to be inherited with the approval of the king, which approval was routinely given. In the 1500s, the king began to allow for the sale of feudal estates. Antonio Cardona decided to sell the Duchy of Alvito in 1592AD to Mateo di Capua, a prince of Conca, for 100,000 ducati. For his investiture in Capua, Mateo di Capua outfitted 150 men from the Duchy and ordered them to accompany him to the city, leaving many peasant families alone and unprotected from the violence of brigands roving the countryside. Those same brigands continued to cause trouble for Mateo and may have been the reason he decided to sell the Duchy, in 1595AD, to Count Matteo Taverna of Milan. Interestingly, the purchase price of 150,000 ducati was actually advanced by Cardinal Tolomeo Gallio - the real purchaser of the Duchy.

Gallio Family. The Gallio family were the feudal lords of the Duchy of Alvito, including Picinisco, from 1595AD through 1806AD.

Cardinal Tolomeo Gallio   Duke from 1595 – 1607. Cardinal Gallio was an important, wealthy man in the Catholic Church who owned many properties, primarily in the north of Italy, near Como. (He was responsible for building the Villa d'Este on Lake Como which was completed in 1570AD). Before he was age forty, he had become a bishop, an archbishop and then a cardinal in 1565AD. He also served as the private secretary of Pope Pius IV and the papal secretary of state to Pope Gregory XIII. At the time he bought the Duchy of Alvito, he was serving as the Bishop of Frascati, but was nearing the end of his long and active career in the Church. He actually bought the Duchy for his beloved nephew Tolomeo, but it was the Cardinal who retained responsibility for the Duchy until his death.

The Cardinal was the first feudal lord to actually be concerned with the welfare of those who lived in the Duchy and, unlike previous dukes, was determined to actively assist in improving their condition. He first visited the Duchy in 1595AD and his biggest concern was with the violence and harassment in the area by local brigands. He stayed for some time in the Duchy and set about improving the situation by codifying ancient laws of the region that helped the peasantry, getting rid of the previously appointed governors in favor of a council of local citizens appointed to administer laws within the Duchy, and establishing local militias to protect the citizens from the brigands. The Cardinal was very fond of the people of the Duchy and contributed some of his own vast resources to make improvements in the region such as new convents, a hospital, fisheries, etc. He made a point of visiting the Duchy every summer and brought his nephew to instruct him in the best manner of handling local affairs. He was deeply mourned by the citizens of the Duchy when he died in 1607.

Tolomeo I   1607 – 1613. The next Gallio to be the Duke of Alvito was the Cardinal's nephew Tolomeo I. Tolomeo I inherited many of his uncle's properties owing to the warm relationship between the two. The Cardinal had taken his eleven-year-old nephew under his wing in 1575AD when his father (the Cardinal's brother Marco Gallio) died. By the time the Cardinal died, Tolomeo I was married with a family of his own and living on one of the family's vast estates in Como. Although his primary interest lay in the north, Tolomeo I followed the Cardinal's instructions to be attentive and fair to his subjects and to treat them with kindness and fatherly love. His early death and lack of documentation about his stewardship of the Duchy makes it difficult to elaborate on his contributions to the town.

Francesco I   1613 – 1657. Francesco was the only son of Tolomeo I and inherited all his father's vast wealth. Francesco, a nobleman like his father, served in the military and eventually became a general in the north of Italy and an ambassador for the King of Spain. He married and had six children and resided at the family home in Como to attend his vast landholdings there. Like his father and grand-uncle, he made many improvements to the Duchy (including minting the first coin of the region in 1619, depicting a bust of himself). But unlike his ancestors, Francesco's primary goal was to improve his own financial situation. His largest source of income from the Duchy came from concessions (permission) he granted to those operating mills on the rivers. Determining that more money could be made were he to own the mills outright, Francesco set about buying all the mills on the river, thereby creating a monopoly. He managed to gain the approval of the town council for his purchases by agreeing to donate a portion of the mill income back to the town coffers, which income was then administered by the same council that approved his acquisitions, a blatant example of the kind of collusion that sometimes existed between the feudal lord and the town council.

Tolomeo II   1657 – 1685. By the time Tolomeo II inherited the Duchy, he was already a 40-year-old man with an important military career in the north of Italy. Initially, he continued pursuing his career in the north, visiting the Duchy only rarely - even after its population was devastated by famine and plague in the 1660s. However, in the 1680s, he moved to Naples and began taking a greater interest in the Duchy. At that time he undertook many projects: building and restoring churches and convents, the construction of a new and important bridge over the River Melfa, reconstruction of the road between Atina and Cassino, and adding new mills and a leatherworks factory.

Francesco II   1685 - 1702. Francesco II was born in Milan and lived the life of a nobleman with his father's legacy. He was characterized by the subjects of his Duchy as "a vicious man of evil mind," said to be cynical, ruthless and arrogant. Duke Francesco II was pressured by Spanish leaders in Naples to provide them with financial support for Spanish war costs and, like many of the nobility, turned to those living in the Duchy, who had few resources of their own, for the extra money. With the Duke in control, the peasants of the Duchy had no recourse against his demands. Perpetually in debt, the families of Picinisco were left in dire straits and the Duke did nothing to alleviate the situation.

Tolomeo Saverio III   1702 - 1711. Tolomeo III inherited the Duchy at the age of 18 but only lived to the age of 26 so his influence in the area was very limited. When he married on July 19, 1708 in Naples, the famous composer George Frederick Handel created a piece called "Aci, Galatea e Polifemo" for his wedding. He lived in Naples and had only one child, Francesco.

Francesco III Trivulzio   1711 - 1749. Because Francesco III was only a child when his father died, it was his uncle, Nicolo Gallio who controlled the Duchy from 1711 to 1727. The region grew in prosperity during his tenure, but perhaps more because of royal laws attempting to reform the conduct of abusive feudal landowners rather than anything that Francesco did while in power. Like his father, Francesco died relatively young, at the age of 39, in Naples.

Carlo Tolomeo Trivulzio IV   1749 – 1800. Carlo was still very young when his father died and his mother Caterina acted as his guardian until 1760. Carlo lived in Naples and eventually sold off many of his family's holdings in northern Italy. He was said to have been an arrogant man who once stated: "there is nothing a baron cannot get from his fief! If he says that donkeys can fly, a thousand people will be ready to testify to it." His reaction to the famine of 1763/64 was to increases taxes on his subjects and he cruelly ignored the starving inhabitants of the Comino Valley.

Francesco Saverio Carafa   1800 - 1806. When Carlo Tolomeo Trivulzio died, his sister's husband, Francesco, inherited the Duchy. Napoleon's decision to end feudal ownership made Francesco's governance as a feudal lord quite brief. He remained in control of property still owned by the family and made unreasonable demands on the peasants for money and goods he was not entitled to, provoking much hatred for his actions in the community.

Carlo Pignatelli, Duke of Montecalvo   1806 - 1813. Carlo was the husband of Marianna Gallio and really acted only as an administrator of the few remaining Gallio properties.

Napoleonic Reforms.   In 1799, Napoleon descended on the Kingdom of Naples and established a republic. Early in the 1800s, a series of reforms were enacted that changed every aspect of Italian society. Feudalism was abolished, causing the Gallio family to lose their power over the Duchy. To reduce the power of the Catholic Church, church properties were confiscated and later sold to raise money for the government. Common lands were divided between the Gallio family and the comune of Picinisco in hopes that they might ultimately be available for sale to the peasants. Primogeniture was abolished so that all heirs had an equal right to share an estate, instead of favoring only the eldest son.

These changes were very difficult to implement and did not necessarily result in the improvement of life for the peasants of Picinisco. Feudal lords fought for years through the court system to keep as much land as possible from their former feudal estates. Local town administrators often manipulated or exploited the common lands, that were now municipal properties, for their personal gain, while peasants lost the use of common lands for grazing. The central government enacted heavy tax burdens that crippled the peasantry. What resulted was a chaotic and uncertain environment for the local population and consequently many peasants in southern Italy grew to mistrust the Napoleonic reforms and were anxious for the return of the Kingdom to a governing party they knew and trusted: the Spanish. In the region of the Comino Valley, groups of brigands organized to attempt to overthrow the Napoleonic government.   However, the political aims of these groups were often overridden by the criminal elements that became associated with the gangs and their violence plagued the existence of those living in the Comino Valley.

The Spanish returned to power over the Kingdom of Two Sicilies (a combination of the formerly separate Kingdoms of Naples and Sicily) in 1815 and ruled for the next 45 years.   Many of the Napoleonic reforms were abandoned with a monarchy again controlling southern Italy, and this angered the emerging liberal political forces there.   The secret society of the Carbonari (freemasonry) arose in this period to push for a republic and other liberal political reforms. These demands were being embraced all over Italy, including a very committed group in the Comino Valley region. The ultimate result was the Risorgimento.

Risorgimento 1860. The Risorgimento (the unification of Italy under a single government) resulted in a particularly violent episode in southern Italian history. Naples were conquered by Giuseppe Garibaldi in 1860 and the entire Kingdom of Two Sicilies joined the new Italian nation in 1861. To insure support for the new national government, the peasants of southern Italy had been promised major land reform measures would be implemented in favor of the poor. However, the new government needed the financial backing of major southern landowners of the day who pressured the new government to abandon any land reforms that would favor the peasants. It took ten more bloody years of fighting in the south of Italy to complete the Risorgimento.

Some southern Italian peasants, angered by their abandonment by the new government, joined forces with the former royal family and their supporters to fight the new order in gangs of brigands. Even those who supported the new national government found their livelihoods threatened by a more modern industrial northern Italy and a national government that neglected the rural southern population. As this rebellion strengthened and the violence intensified, the new government responded with military action. To suppress the notion that the southern uprising was directed against the unification of the country, (and thus a civil war of the south against north), the national government recast the rebellion as "unrest" caused by gangs of brigands. A small National Guard manned by peasant farmers in the south was called upon to root out this "brigand problem". When it was not successful, the new government appointed a military commander in 1865 and assigned more than two-thirds of the Italian army to secure the region. This military intervention was initially successful in forcing the brigands from the more heavily populated regions in the south. However, in the vast, relatively unsettled, mountainous region that included Picinisco the fight (characterized as the "Brigands War" or peasant revolt) continued until 1870. There are estimates regarding the loss of lives during the 10-year period following unification that range from 250,000 to 1 million, though the unified state would prohibit any meaningful gathering of statistics for obvious reasons. In any event, this was a very dangerous and bloody period for the south of Italy and particularly for the Piciniscani.

Province of Frosinone 1927.   Following the Risorgimento, Picinisco was still part of the province of Terra di Lavoro, one of the largest provinces in the newly unified Italy.   In 1927, it was determined to separate this large province into smaller ones. Thus, the comune of Picinisco became part of the Province of Frosinone, in the region of Lazio.

Chapter 3

Evolution of the Landscape

A "fortified" settlement with a "surrounding wall" is how the mountaintop town of Picinisco was first described in 1054AD. The fortification referred to a tower approximately 18 meters tall and almost 13 meters in diameter, with four stories, primarily used for military purposes. The original town wall followed a circular path around the top of the mountain, encompassing the fortified tower, at least two additional watchtowers, and connecting the four gates ("porta," meaning door) providing access to the town. Much of this original architecture is still visible in the town today.

Historians believe that the first residences of the town were located near the gate known as "Porta Saracina." In fact, some believe that this area may have been a small settlement predating the construction of the town's tower and walls. The architecture of this gate is similar to the town's watch-towers that some speculate may have been built as early as the tenth century. The remains of some adjacent residences here suggest an even earlier, pre-incastellamento, settlement may have existed at Porta Saracina. Also, this gate opens on to what was, for hundreds of years, the main route from Picinisco down to the larger, neighboring city of Atina and the rest of the Comino Valley. The name of the gate, the nearby street and alleyway (all having the same name - Saracina) may be attributed to a settlement established just after the Saracen invasion, at the end of the ninth century. So, it is possible that this area was first developed many years before the town was walled in.

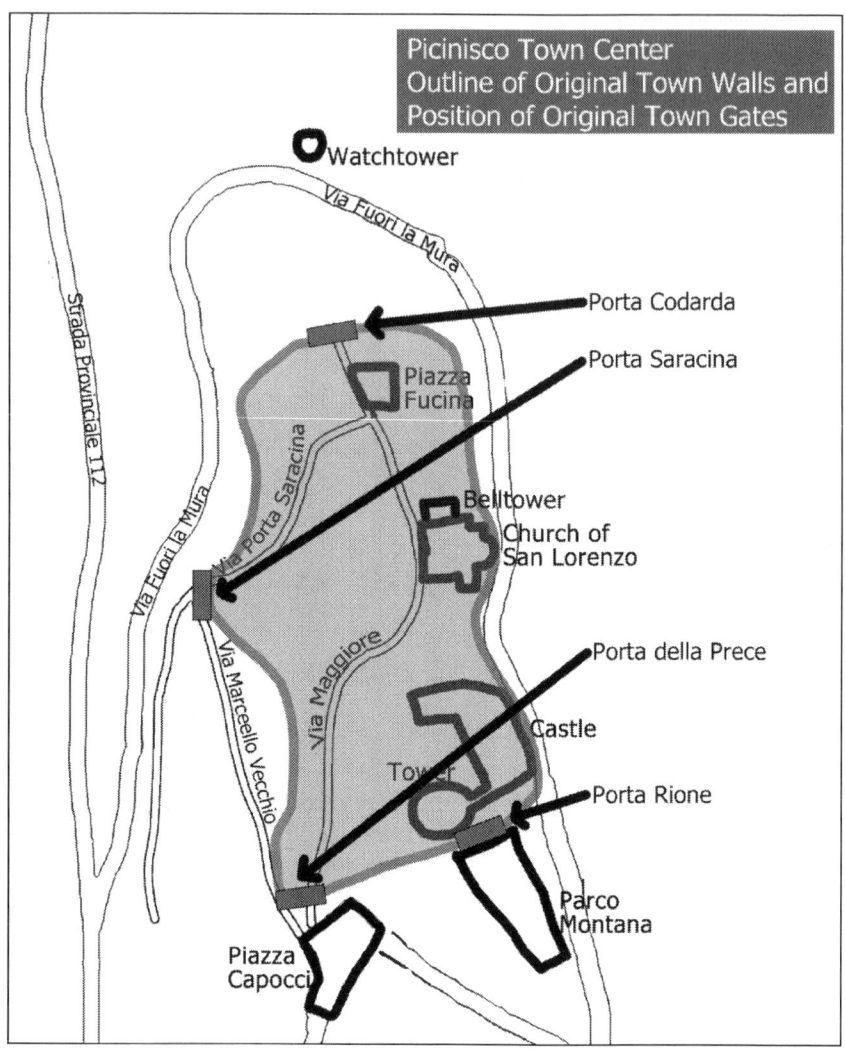

Picinisco Town Center
Outline of Original Town Walls and
Position of Original Town Gates

Watchtower

Via Fuori la Mura

Strada Provinciale 112

Porta Codarda

Porta Saracina

Piazza Fucina

Via Porta Saracina

Via Fuori la Mura

Belltower
Church of
San Lorenzo

Via Maggiore

Via Marcello Vecchio

Porta della Prece

Castle

Tower

Porta Rione

Parco
Montana

Piazza
Capocci

In addition to Porta Saracina, there were three other doors leading into the walled settlement. "Porta della Prece" is located just inside of the archway now existing off Piazza Capocci. This door was previously called "Porta Maggiore" but its name was changed in recognition of the custom of people stopping to pray at the sight of the Church of Santa Maria Assunta, just through the door. "Porta Codarda", located at the northern edge of the town, provides access to Piazza Fucina. "Porta Rione", located next to the castle, leads directly into Parco Montano. The "Porta della Piazza", a fifth door that leads off the main Piazza Capocci and through to the Porta della Prece, was constructed in the eighteenth century. The piazza itself was not originally part of the walled town - the town walls stopped outside of the piazza, at the Porta della Prece.

The watch-towers along the eastern and northern sides of the town walls were certainly present by the time the town wall was built. The watchtower to the east was enclosed as a new bell-tower for the Church of San Lorenzo in about 1300AD. Architecturally, it resembles the watchtower (called the "toretto") that is located outside the town walls to the north, near Porta Codarda. This northern outpost offered a perfect view of the Melfa River as it flowed by Picinisco.

The earliest residences likely expanded from the Porta Saracina area towards the eastern watchtower (that is now the bell-tower of San Lorenzo) and south towards the original fortified tower. These oldest homes were all built with light-colored stone and many used the town wall as the back wall of the house. In these homes, windows and doors were cut into stone that was as thick as two feet. Many of the house doors at the street level were made in the shape of an arch and quite wide enough to have allowed a cart and livestock to move freely into and out of the house. The main streets of the original town were: Via Maggiore (now Via Gustino Ferri, in recognition of one of Picinisco's famous residents), which ran from Piazza Fucina (near Porta Cordado) past the Church of San Lorenzo to the Porta della Prece (near the Piazza Capocci); Via di Porta Saracina, which connected the Piazza Fucina to the Porta di Saracina and ran almost parallel to the Via Maggiore; and Via Marcello Vecchio, which connected the Piazza Capocci with the Porta Saracina. Off these main streets, many small alleyways and staircases were constructed to reach residences wholly within the town walls. The original gardens of the townspeople were located just outside the town walls.

During the first few hundred years of Picinisco's existence, the center of religious activity was outside the town wall, about 1/2 mile down the mountain from the center of town. The Church of Santa Maria Assunta is first mentioned in a document dated in 1110AD, although remnants of a pagan church have been found on this same site. By the 1300s, the Church had a monastery with a dozen priests in residence and served the town of Picinisco and those living in the surrounding countryside. As the town's population grew, new churches were established in new neighborhoods: the Church of San Nicolo was located in the vicinity of the Porta

Codarda (perhaps as early as 1100AD, but certainly by 1300AD), and, just beyond the town wall, new residents of the area called San Croce established the Church of San Croce in the early 1300s. (Both churches are gone now).

The Church of San Lorenzo (now the main church of Picinisco) was built within the walls of the town sometime before 1305, when it is first mentioned in a document found in Catholic Church archives. It began life as a small chapel that was an extension of the Church of Santa Maria Assunta, built to allow the priests to be closer to their congregation within the walls of the town. Over the next two centuries the San Lorenzo chapel was enlarged in size, including the enclosure of the old town watchtower as a bell-tower for the church, and became increasingly important to the community. By the 1500s, it had its own monastery and priests, and was formally recognized as the main religious center of Picinisco. The Church of San Lorenzo also functioned as a municipal hall for the town: according to a document, dated 1546, the Church was used for a meeting of the citizens of Picinisco, to discuss concessions from the feudal lord and to elect the next mayor. Also during the 1500s, what is now the Church of San Rocco, was added in Piazza Capocci.

From the late 1300s to the early 1400s, the feudal lords of the Cantelmo family began extensive renovations on the original main tower within the town walls, enclosing it inside a much larger tower capable of housing residents. This new tower was built in the style of the Castel Nuovo in Naples. The Cantelmo family also built three new towers and connected them to the original tower to form a single castle complex. This new complex was later depicted in the town's crest. The complex was large enough to house a military unit as well as a caretaker and his family. The Cantelmo family also dug a moat around the castle and built two drawbridges to provide access to the castle. These drawbridges were placed near what is now Porta Rione and Via Ponte, and their presence is verified by descriptions of Picinisco written in the late 1500s and early 1600s. Water was available to town residents from the Scopella Fountain, located just outside the town walls, or from the fountain at the Church of Santa Maria Assunta. The first mention of the cemetery next to the Church of Santa Maria Assunta is found in 1592.

In the 1600s, the Gallio family commissioned stucco panels of each of the towns in the Duchy and we can see from the Picinisco stucco that by this time the town had expanded well beyond the original walls. Because of the topography of the mountaintop, there was really no place to put new residences other than toward the south, down from the top of the mountain toward the Church of Santa Maria Assunta. The Piazza Capocci was clearly in place at this time, though it was much smaller and narrower.

In the early 1700s, a large municipal building, designed in the baroque style, was completed outside of the Porta della Prece, on the edge of Piazza Capocci. The castle also underwent extensive renovation at this time: it was enlarged to include the large L-shaped structure now called the "Palazzo Ducale". (A palazzo indicates it had become more of a palace than just a fortified castle). At the turn of the century, as some prosperity was enjoyed by the townspeople, artisans were employed to adorn the large arched doorways of their residences with coats of arms, special keystone decorations and other symbols and sometimes the name of the resident. Other residents had balconies crafted in stone or iron added to their homes. The Church of San Lorenzo also changed in appearance as a new facade was added.

By the early 1800s, the town had become a busy commercial center: three cantinas/bars, two grocery stores, a school, a butcher, a blacksmith, cobbler, a post and telegraph office and a police station with three policemen had been established. In 1812, following the abolishment of feudal ownership, the Bartolomucci family became the first private owners of the Palazzo Ducale. The family's profitable dairy, olive oil operation and nearby paper mill were run from an agency located in Largo Rione (the open space in front of the castle and Palazzo Ducale complex). Their paper mill was maintained in the community of Borgo Castellone, down the mountain from Picinisco. The large plane tree in Piazza Capocci was first planted in the early 1800s and the Church of San Rocco was established (from the remains of an older church) at about the same time. The new entryway of the Porta della Piazza, with its clock-towers and arches connected to the baroque building of the 1700s, was completed in 1838. By the end of the century, in 1898, the first hydraulically-powered electrical plant was constructed on the River Melfa, bringing electricity to the town in 1911. The main piazza was dedicated to the famous Piciniscani astronomer, Ernesto Capocci, in 1890.

In 1911, the castle was designated as a landmark by the Italian government.   Unfortunately, in the large earthquake of 1915 portions of the castle were damaged and had to be torn down. The area outside the castle, which was previously known as "Il Montano" and then "Largo Montano", became Parco Montano. The area was terraced and landscaped as park and a monument was erected to those who had died in World War I and later modified to include those who died in World War II. New fountains were built in the Capocci and Fucina piazzas and in Parco Montana in the 1920s, with water channeled from the Scopella Fountain. In 1922, the Parco Nazionale d'Abruzzo, Lazio e Molise was founded and an entrance was located in the town of Picinisco. Many emigrants returned to Picinisco in the early 1900s and began major restorations to their family homes, as well as new building efforts. One such person was Orazio Cervi, who built a large Victorian villa in the community of Serre where he hosted the famous author D.H. Lawrence and his wife Frieda in 1919.

During World War II, Picinisco was directly hit by bombs in January, 1944. Damage to the town center took years to repair and damage done to the main tower of the castle is still awaiting repair. The Church of Santa Maria Assunta had to be substantially repaired as well.   Roads were mined and property destroyed as part of the German occupation of the town. Following the devastation of the war, the town rebuilt but its population declined and less commercial activity was found in the center. New buildings were constructed in the 1950s to house a grammar school and a hotel serving the National Park. Significant rebuilding was necessary again after the earthquake of 1984 that did considerable damage to the town.   More recently, the town has become revitalized as a tourist center, offering visitors delightful new accommodations to enjoy the fantastic views from the historic center and the natural wonders of the Comino Valley. Looking up from the valley below, the town sparkles as the sun catches the light-colored buildings perched atop the mountain among the greenery and larger mountains that frame its position.

Frazioni/Hamlets.   As the historic center of Picinisco was changing, so too was the surrounding countryside. Several small outlying hamlets, called "frazioni," became part of the Picinisco territory. The earliest of them to have been settled was "Immoglie," where the monastery of San Valentino was located in 894AD. It lies to the south of Picinisco and sits at an altitude of 550 meters above sea level. The name is believed to have come from "la moglia" (wife), used to describe the particularly fertile terrain there. Although the original monastery was apparently abandoned by the 1300s and lay in complete ruins by the 1500s, a small number of inhabitants stayed in this area.

Evidence of the existence of a church in an outlying area allows assumptions about the timing of the establishment of various other frazioni. In a document describing a visit of the Bishop of Sora to Picinisco in 1305, several churches are noted. The Church of San Giovanni di Prato is identified in a location between Valleporcina and Fontitune. Both of these communities lie directly east of Picinisco, at much higher elevations: Valleporcina at 820 meters and Fontitune at 952 meters above sea level. In fact, Fontitune is the town with the highest elevation in all of the National Park of Abruzzo, Lazio and Molise. Valleporcina has also been called "Colle Porcina" and its name is likely a reference to the wild pigs plentiful in this higher elevation. Fontitune was previously called "Fonteluna," which roughly translates to "the source of the moon," possibly a reference to its particularly high elevation. This Church of San Giovanni di Prato (in early inventories of Church properties the area was called "San Janni") likely served a community of shepherds while they grazed their flocks on the upper mountains in summer. Church inventories dated in the late 1500s suggest there were year-round residents living there by then.

Also included among the churches in the 1305 document is the Church of San Pietro, located between the frazioni of Casale and Colleruta. Both of these small towns lie south and a bit west of Picinisco at elevations of around 680 meters above sea level. Interestingly, all traces of the Church of San Pietro disappear by the mid-1300s. They do not appear again until 1588 when property in "Colle Della Ruta" is mentioned as part of some church properties under lease.

The Churches of San Giovanni and San Antonio, located at La Rocca, existed in 1305 as well. La Rocca was at this time called

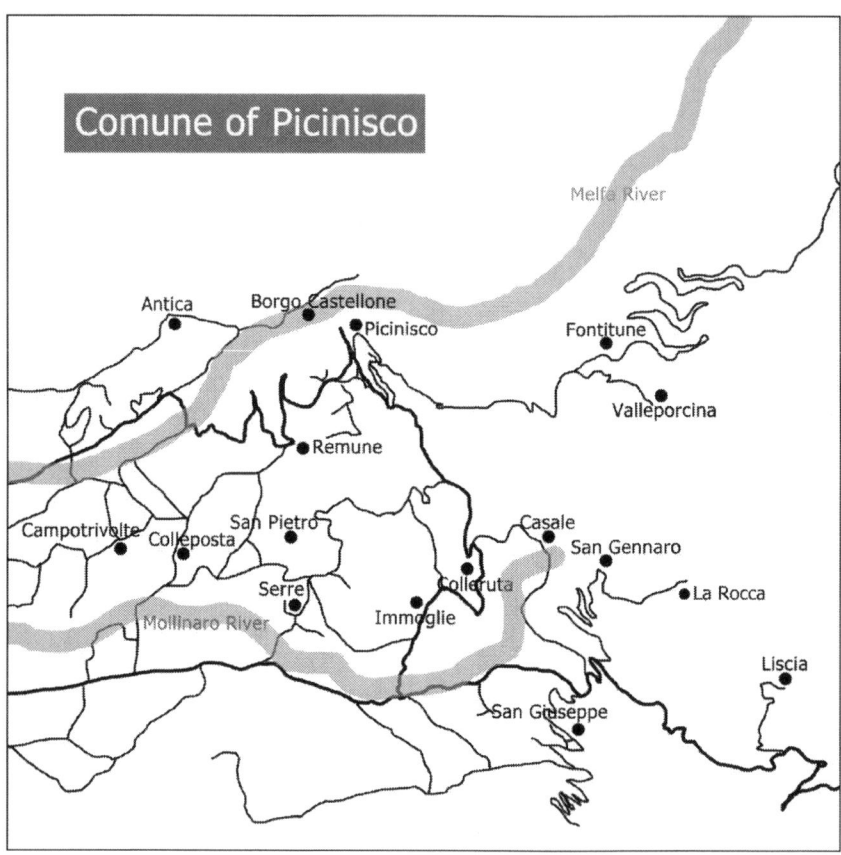

"Rocca Albano" or "Monte Albano" and was a separate feudal property belonging to Roberto Ingresso, perhaps as early as 1100. The castle at Rocca Albano was destroyed in 1435 by Riccio di Montechiaro. In 1546, the area was renamed "Rocca degli Alberi" when it became part of the feudal property of the Duchy of Alvito. It stands at approximately 914 meters above sea level.

The communities of San Pietro, Serre and Mole di Vito all have churches established in the 1600s. San Pietro was formerly known as Santa Petro. The church established there in the late 1600s was called San Pietro sul Colle Martorello. However, the community may have already been in residence as early as 1615, according to an earlier Church inventory.   Serre's church, Santa Maria di Constantinople, was founded in 1689. Serre's elevation is at 497 meters above sea level, on top of a rise just south of Picinisco. It was formerly known as "Rocca Della Quatro Norre." Closer to the valley, at a much lower elevation, to the west of Picinisco is Mole di Vito, at 390 meters. A watermill built there in 1613 by one of the Gallio family confirms its existence then as well.

Churches in the communities of San Gennaro (formerly known as "Aia del Lupo" and "Ara dei Lupi") and San Giuseppe were established in the 1700s. Lupo is Italian for "wolf" which likely roamed the high altitude of San Gennaro's location at 831 meters. Interestingly, Picinisco author Ernesto Capocci's book entitled "Il Primo Viceré di Napoli" describes "Aia del Lupo" as a village existing in the early 1500s. San Giuseppe, previously known as Colaguardia or Colle della Guardia, lies in the southernmost part of Picinisco's territory, along the Mollarino river.

Some historians suggest that the Church of San Giusta, located in the community of Antica, was also founded in the 1300s, although there is no actual written record of the community until a Catholic Church inventory dated in 1615. Antica lies at 502 meters above sea level and is located directly west of Picinisco. Other frazioni in existence at the time of the 1615 church inventory include Chiuselle (previously known as La Chiusella), Colleposta (previously known as Colle della Posta), Remune and Campotrivolte (previously known as Campo Trivolto).

Chapter 4

Feudal Power and Local Government

In 1017AD, Picinisco's residents were subject to the control of the local nobility, the Marsi family. The crown in Naples was too far away to exert effective control over isolated communities like Picinisco, so the local nobility stepped in, backed by their own militia. Eventually, as the feudal estate system developed, the feudal lord stood in the shoes of the King in Naples vis a vis the Picinisco residents. However, one of the objectives of the incastellamento period during which Picinisco was founded was to allow the community to have a leadership structure to address purely local concerns. By the twelfth century, a structure emerged in the form of a municipal association called a "università" that could function within the developing system of feudal power. The università endured for hundreds of years and became the foundation for the "comune" form of government, adopted after Italian unification in 1861, and still in existence today.

The università was comprised of a group of citizens charged with regulating purely local affairs. Quasi-democratic in nature, the università initially operated like the guilds of medieval times: free men in the community (male heads of households) voted to elect the members of the università and to determine the rules that would apply to the community and then everyone agreed to be bound by those rules for the betterment of the group. The università elected a mayor, often a lawyer or notary, from among its members. It met regularly and meetings were open to the community. The first written record of the Università in Picinisco is dated November 30, 1546 and describes a meeting held at the Church of San Lorenzo to elect the mayor of Picinisco - Iacobuccio di Antonio Santangeli.

The most important responsibilities of the Università were dealing with the "common lands" in Picinisco and apportioning the burden of the taxes/fees owed to the crown in Naples and to the feudal lord. Common lands were shared by the community and available to everyone for pasturing, forestry and the like, according to local custom. The group determined the appropriate use and charges for common lands and dealt with controversies among users - trying to maintain a balance between resources and the needs of the community.   Apportioning taxes/fees required the Università to determine who was capable of paying and how much they could afford to pay. The Università made regular payments to the feudal lord and, less regularly, to the crown in Naples. They were entitled to grant exemptions to those who were poor, provided the number did not exceed a minimal percentage of the total population. The Church was completely exempt from taxation until the Napoleonic reforms of the early 1800s and thus contributed nothing to payments due to the feudal lord or the crown. When the crown did impose taxes, the feudal lord typically passed his share along to the rest of the community.   So, to a large degree, taxes were apportioned among the peasantry.

The Università of Picinisco also dealt with the università of neighboring towns on behalf of the community. For example, in the 1500s they responded to an accusation by the Università of Atina that people from Picinisco had built a wall within Atina's borders to stop Atina farmers from planting new vines there. In the 1600s, the Picinisco Università negotiated with the Università of Atina to determine fees imposed on traveling merchants participating in their local markets and the security of roads from menacing gangs of brigands. The Università employed professionals on behalf of the town, paying the salaries of a doctor, an attorney and others working for the community. In terms of financial resources, the Università collected local fees and taxes, revenue from the use of communal property and revenue from property owned by the Università and leased to others. In terms of expenditures, the Università was obligated to maintain common lands, pay administrative salaries, ensure the town's security, and make payments to the feudal lord in satisfaction of his fees.

In theory, the feudal lord was excluded from all business of the università, but in practice the entitlements of feudal ownership caused constant friction. The power of feudal ownership came not just from the ownership of tracts of land, but from a list of rights, privileges and monopolies that attached to the area within the feudal boundaries. In fact, in most cases, those rights, privileges and monopolies brought in considerably more revenue to the feudal lord than did his land. And those same rights, privileges and monopolies created opportunities for the feudal owner to exploit the università in many different ways.

At the beginning of the feudal system, the feudal lord was completely responsible for criminal and civil jurisdiction within his feudal estate, meaning he appointed all the judges (and sometimes even the appellate-level judges) trying matters involving the citizenry of the feud. Thus, any controversy between a feudal lord and the Università (or any resident of Picinisco) was destined to be resolved in favor of the feudal lord. The feudal lord was also entitled to appoint all officers of the crown, such as the bailiff, the person in charge of weights and measures, buildings inspectors, toll and tax collectors, etc. The right to make these official appointments was "sold" to the Picinisco Università for a fee that had to be negotiated with the Università. The feudal lord had monopolies on various businesses such as mills, communal ovens, inns, hunting and fishing, etc. and was entitled to payment by anyone engaged in such activities. People living within the feud could be called upon for certain services to the lord, such as protection of his castle or other property, or be forced to pay a tax to avoid such service. The feudal lord had a right to collect fees for the use of any property he owned outright as well.

Feudal lords, and their representative local governors in southern Italy, sometimes attempted to interfere with the membership of a università to enhance their own economic returns. They tried to influence who was elected to the università by calling for elections without notifying the entire voting population. They were known to bribe members of a università. They interfered with the università's determination of who could pay taxes and how much they would pay. They negotiated exemptions from taxation for themselves and their wealthy supporters. In the late 1600s, feudal lords began to look for more than just an income stream from their holdings and began to engage in their own manufacturing and trade. If required, they would manipulate a università to approve transactions for their benefit, as did Francesco Gallio when he achieved a monopoly over all mills in Picinisco in the 1600s.

The tension between the feudal landowner and università continued until the demise of feudal ownership in the early 1800s. The king in Naples refereed the relationship between them depending upon his own needs and concerns. When the king needed the nobility to supply money or soldiers, or to approve his appointment of a successor, his decrees favored the feudal lords and expanded their powers over the università. When the nobility threatened the king, the king punished them by calling for reforms that supported the independence of the università, both in terms of their interactions with the feudal lord (for example, requiring contracts between a università and the feudal lord to be approved by the king) and their internal operations (for example, insuring the members of a università were duly elected by the citizenry). In the last hundred years of feudal power, the crown began to allow the università to accumulate financial resources of its own and elect an independent judiciary. Once this was accomplished, a università was able to address disputes with the feudal lord in the courts and enforce their control over local matters. By the end of the 1700s, the Università in Picinisco was in a much stronger position to assert its authority and began challenging the Gallio family successfully in court.

When Napoleon arrived in Naples, he decided that economic prosperity could only be achieved if the antiquated feudal ownership system was abolished and peasants were allowed to own their own land. Napoleonic reforms, particularly the new code of justice, maintained and strengthened the position of the università until the creation of the new state of Italy in 1861. Picinisco's Università ultimately became a "comune" and assumed full control over the operations of the community, reporting to the provincial government in Frosinone and ultimately to the national government.

Today, the comune is led by a mayor (sindaco), deputy mayor, and a town council, elected by the town's population, including anyone age 18 or older. It is responsible for public health concerns, transport, registries of births, marriages and deaths, and property transfers in the comune. The comune can collect taxes and receives money from the central government for local services like roads, schools, sewage, water supply, and rubbish pick-up. It also maintains a municipal police force.

Chapter 5

Population

Today the comune of Picinisco has a population of 1200. Approximately 300 of these individuals reside in the mountaintop town and the rest can be found in the smaller hamlets of the comune. Historical population data for Picinisco is reliable for the years beginning with Italy's establishment as a single unified state, in 1861. Before that time, the numbers are much less accurate.

Medieval population censuses in the Kingdom of Naples were undertaken solely for reasons of taxation. The earliest taxes were imposed based on a hearth ("fuoco"), or household, rather than a per capita census. Because many groups were exempted from taxation (e.g. paupers, widows, the church and sometimes the nobility), even the exact number of households was indeterminable. The earliest population figure reported by Picinisco to the King in Naples was 146 households, in 1532. To give this figure some perspective, there were approximately 40,000 households in the city of Naples in 1532, 1000 in Capua (the second largest city of Terra di Lavoro) and 320 in Gaeta (the third largest). In 1545, Picinisco reported 160 households and in 1561, 193 households.

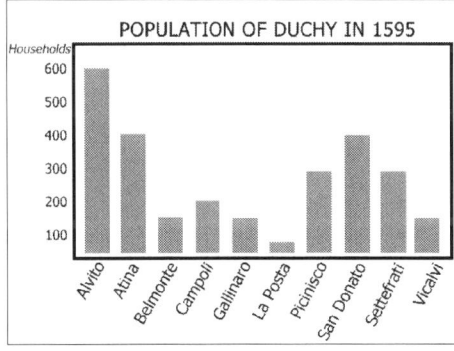

In 1595, a report was written for Cardinal Gallio upon his purchase of the Duchy of Alvito which included an assessment of the population of each of the ten towns of the Duchy. In that year, there were a total of 300 households reported for Picinisco. This large increase over the population of 1561 may be attributable to the fact that this 1595 assessment was a description of the area for the new owner, so the author may have determined to include some households (religious, paupers, etc.) who were normally left off the tax rolls.

Between the years 1648 and the next taxation census in 1669, there was a 35% drop in the number of households reported in Picinisco (from 273 to 180 households). This very large reduction in the population is likely explained by the arrival of the plague in the Comino Valley in 1656. During the 1700s through the mid-1800s population figures were gradually changed from "households" to per capita calculations and the population of Picinisco stayed fairly constant, at approximately 3,000 people over this period. In the first national per capita census after the formation of the modern Italian state in 1861, 3,275 people were reported in the comune of Picinisco. Ten years later in 1871 the number had risen to 3,806 and, for the first time, the census included a breakdown of the population of the town of Picinisco and at least some of the surrounding hamlets: Picinisco - approximately 1200, Fontitune - 319, San Gennaro - 597, San Giuseppe - 448, Serre - 439, San Pietro - 509 and Antica - 264.

Between the 1870s and the 1880s the population dropped by 300 people.   This drop reflects the first wave of emigration from Picinisco that occurred in response to a decline in the economic situation and the violence suffered by the region.   Twenty years later, in the 1901 census, the population of Picinisco dropped again to 2,563 people, reflecting further emigration.   That 1901 census also offered a breakdown for the many of the hamlets of Picinisco: Picinisco - 640, Fontitune - 122, Valleporcina - 72, Casale - 87, Casalnera - 35, Chiuselle - 55, San Gennaro - 75, La Rocca - 80, Liscia - 121, Matura - 104, San Giuseppe - 147, Immoglie - 64, Colleruta - 81, Serre - 121, Valleoscura - 59, San Pietro - 116, Colleposta - 158, Collepanico - 107, Campotrivolte – 89, and Antica - 230.

Interestingly, Picinisco's closest neighboring town, Settefrati, suffered the same population decline between 1881 and 1901. In fact, throughout the period of the national Italian census, every ten years from 1861 to 2011, the population graphs of Picinisco and Settefrati are very nearly identical, suggesting their proximity resulted in similar economic situations and responses. This was not the case with respect to Picinisco's other neighbors: in the remaining eight towns that were originally part of the Duchy of Alvito, seven actually made fairly significant population gains between 1881 and 1901, except Vicalvi, which suffered a small loss.

During the first twenty years of the 1900s, the population of Picinisco climbed again to 3,837. It is possible that this rise in population is attributable to a number of temporary emigrants who returned to the area after achieving a level of economic prosperity abroad. The Italian government estimates that as many as half of those who left Italy after unification in 1861 may have actually returned to the country. Following the two world wars and another wave of emigration, the population in Picinisco stabilized at approximately 2500. In the 1950s, another 500 people left Picinisco and the population declined to about 1900. Beginning in the 1960s, the population steadily declined to its present-day level of 1200. In comparison, the present-day populations of the other towns of the Duchy are as follows: Atina - 4500, Alvito - 2850, San Donato - 2122, Campoli - 1750, Gallinaro - 1246, Posta Fibreno - 1217, Settefrati - 792, Belmont - 778, and Vicalvi - 492.

Chapter 6

Travel and Transportation

From the time Picinisco was founded, there were streets inside the walls connecting the various gates and piazzas. Most were wide enough to accommodate an animal and cart and were paved with stone. Smaller paths and staircases accommodated residences at different elevations. These same passageways are still in existence today; some have been modified to accommodate automobile traffic, while others have been left in their original state.

Traveling to and from the town center was a much more challenging endeavor, for literally hundreds of years. The earliest transit routes up and down the mountain were likely forged by herds of sheep going to and from summer mountain pastures above Picinisco, perhaps before Picinisco was even founded. The main entrance to the town was through the Porta Saracina gate, rather than into the piazza, as is the case today. A well-worn switch-back trail led down the mountain from there to the Church of Santa Maria Assunta. Further down the mountain, the trail linked up with the Via Mole di Vito, which led from the bottom of the mountain towards the town of Atina. Atina, founded many hundreds of years before Picinisco, was strategically positioned along an ancient trade route that offered access to the outside world.

Atina was an important center of weapons production in early Roman times, largely because of its access to Mt. Meta (located behind Picinisco) and the iron that could be mined there. A well-travelled route existed running south from Atina to the larger city of Cassino (then called San Germano), which was situated along the early Roman road called the "Via Latina," connecting Rome to southern Italy. The same route also ran north from Atina to the town of Sora, a town also colonized by the early Romans, located on the banks of the River Liri. During the first several hundred years of Picinisco's existence this well-traveled Sora-to-Cassino route was still just a trail traversed on foot or by mule. Carriages did not come into wider use in the Kingdom of Naples until the late 1500s. It was not until well into the 1700s that the crown in Naples began to focus attention and investment on the interior roads of the

Kingdom. The renewed interest in mining operations in the Comino Valley prompted the completion of a properly graded road running from Sora all the way to Naples in the 1790s.

Apart from the physical condition of these routes in and around the Comino Valley, travel involved other complications. Travel was very dangerous because of the presence of gangs of brigands based in the nearby mountains. Many historians refer to the risk of robbery as well as physical harm from these bandits, beginning as early as the 1500s. Even into the late 1700s and early 1800s, travel guides written by those on "grand tours" of Italy warned tourists about these gangs. In order to provide protection to travelers and to maintain the road system, tolls were charged for the use of these routes. Initially, in areas far away from the capital in Naples, feudal lords assumed responsibility for the road system through their local governors. This created massive confusion as the system of tolls was as varied as the number of feudal estates a traveler needed to cross. As early as the 1400s, the crown in Naples tried to assert control over the interior road system to allow freer trade. However, feudal owners fought back claiming the right to charge travelers crossing their lands was part of their feudal privileges. The number of recorded tolls in the Kingdom of Naples grew from around 30 in 1469 to over 800 by the late 1600s. Eventually, local governments also began financing roads and bridges and posting security on roadways, adding to the chaos. One of Napoleon's major reform measures in the early 1800s was to abolish all tolls and regularize the roadway system. In addition to the dangers and cost of travel, the Kingdom of Naples protected its borders with checkpoints designed to ensure that all desiring to enter or leave the Kingdom had the proper permissions or visas. Once the country was unified as a single state, passports were issued to all Italian citizens permitting a freer flow of traffic.

The route between Picinisco and Atina was still described as a "rough trail" and a "bridal path" into the early 1800s. The Bartolomucci family, owners of a successful paper mill at Borgo Castellone at the base of the Picinisco mountaintop, set about improving the road from there to Atina around 1820. "Improvement" meant grading and widening the road for transportation of goods. By the 1890s, an English guidebook described the route as a "good road of 6 miles." Early in the 1900s, then mayor of Picinisco, Ernesto Boni, spearheaded a campaign for a new road from the hamlet of Remune at the base of the Picinisco mountaintop to San Pietro and Colle Posta, and eventually to Villa Latina, providing the

Piciniscani with another route to Atina. He was also responsible for widening roads to accommodate vehicular traffic.

In 1919, the famous author D.H. Lawrence made a journey to Picinisco from Rome. He describes taking the train from Rome to Cassino, a route first available in the 1870s. (Still today, the nearest train depot to Picinisco is in Cassino). In Cassino, Lawrence transferred to a bus for Atina. In the 1920s, this Cassino-to-Sora bus service added a regular stop in Picinisco, but was not yet in service when Lawrence was travelling. From Atina, Lawrence went by cart along a graded, unpaved road to within a mile of his destination in the Picinisco hamlet of Serre. The last part of his trip had to be made on foot. That same year, while staying in Serre, Lawrence visited Picinisco and described the route from Serre to Picinisco as a "sheer scramble - no road whatever."

The Piciniscani who lived in the town during World War II describe roadways covered in white limestone, enabling the residents of Picinisco to easily observe approaching vehicles.   One author observed that during the war there were only three private automobiles in the entire town, although many German vehicles travelled the road from Atina to Picinisco during the war. The main road between Picinisco and Atina was finally paved in the 1950s.

After Italian unification in the 1860s, the national government began working on major roadways and assigned responsibility for provincial and local roadways among the respective governmental bodies.   In 1956, the national government started building a highway called the "Autostrada del Sole" running from Milan to Naples. An exit at Cassino provided access to the Comino Valley. The route from Cassino to Atina (about 18 kilometers - up and over the mountaintop at Belmonte Castello) was about an hour-long drive through the end of the 1980s.   State highway 509 "Forca d'Acero," which runs from the town of Opi in the National Park of Abruzzo, Molise and Lazio, down through San Donato Valcomino, was built in the late 1800s. However, it was not until the 1990s that this highway was extended to Atina and all the way to Cassino. Today the drive from Atina to Cassino takes less than 20 minutes.

Chapter 7

Economic Activity

Picinisco's first settlers were part of an agrarian-pastoral economy that was based entirely on self-consumption. They either grew grains, tended orchards, vineyards and olive groves, took care of animals and produced cheese, milk, eggs and meat, or collected money from tenants and employees who performed such services. For those who did not own land, the fruits of their labor went first to the landowner and what was left was exchanged for the goods they needed. Some skilled tradesmen useful to the activities of agriculture and pasturage were part of the community (i.e. tool-makers, millers, etc.), but the vast majority of the people relied on themselves for whatever they needed to make their livings. Their "market" involved trading with neighbors for anything they did not make themselves. In Picinisco, this market reflected the symbiotic relationship between the farmer and the shepherd: Picinisco offered proximity to both activities making it largely economically autonomous. This simple market economy lasted for literally hundreds of years and kept the peasantry at a subsistence level, while the landowners collected their due.

The only real surplus of goods from this early simple economy belonged to the landowners (the feudal lord, the church and a few wealthy individuals) and their ability to market goods was severely limited by the profound difficulties of transportation, well into the nineteenth century. Goods had to be carried off the mountain by individuals or pack animals (a mule team of 6 to 7 animals could carry about one ton of goods). Regional "fairs" held in Alvito (the capital of the Duchy), beginning in the 1460s and in Atina, beginning in the 1550s, were wholesale markets held several times a year to attract buyers from larger urban areas. Unlike the landowners, the peasant population traded among themselves at the weekly Sunday market in Picinisco and sold any excess goods in the larger weekly market in Atina.

The primary economic objective of feudal landowners in the middle ages was to secure a steady stream of income that could support their lifestyle in the capital in Naples. Profit required personal effort and capital investment that most feudal landowners were not interested in making. The first significant investment in Picinisco during the first several hundred years of its existence came from the Cantelmo family, when they expanded the castle complex during the late 1300s and early 1400s. However, when the Gallio family bought the Duchy of Alvito in 1595, they took a personal interest in the local affairs of the Duchy and its inhabitants. The Gallios invested their own capital in the Duchy in many different ways, but none more important than the investment they made in transportation. Building bridges and improving security for merchants traveling in the Duchy permitted the movement of goods to larger markets. Like other feudal lords of the 1600s, the Gallio family began to shift their economic objective to secure new sources of income from their feud, and invested in businesses directly, rather than simply collecting income. They purchased and created new mills along the rivers, not just for grinding grain but for mechanizing textile and paper production. Economic opportunities emerged for the construction trades as the Gallios provided funding for major building and restoration projects. They invested in the exploitation of natural resources and provided opportunities for those skilled in forestry and later mining. These new enterprises needed a labor force which attracted more people to Picinisco, in turn creating more jobs in local government to meet the needs of the rising population.

The measures taken by the early lords of the Gallio family helped set Picinisco on a course that would improve the economic situation for its residents. During the mid-1600s, circumstances interrupted this forward momentum: severe weather caused significant crop damage, the crown imposed increasing taxes to finance the Thirty Years War, and population declines resulting from the plague caused Picinisco's economy to suffer. But, by the 1700s, employment opportunities were on the rise again, improved transportation and new markets for goods were opened, and some townspeople were able to buy land and establish businesses formerly monopolized by the feudal lord and the Church. Feudal monopolies began to be challenged successfully in court. More people had enough money to educate their children. With the abolition of feudalism and the confiscation of Church property at the beginning of the 1800s, even more people were able to secure private property and enjoy some economic success. Picinisco became quite a bustling center of economic activity during this period.

Unfortunately, this economic prosperity did not last. The industrial revolution in Italy eventually caused prices for many of the goods produced in Picinisco to fall. The period leading up to the formation of a single Italian state was characterized by violent unrest in the south of Italy, particularly in Picinisco where they were constantly under attack by local brigands. The abolition of primogeniture (inheritance by the eldest son) resulted in the division of farms into smaller and smaller plots, incapable of supporting a family. Once Italy was unified in 1861, the southern population faced heavier taxation with less land for production. At this point, many chose to leave Picinisco to seek opportunity in a more favorable economic environment. More than anything, this exodus of the population had a devastating effect on Picinisco's economy at the end of the nineteenth century.

At the turn of the twentieth century, some Piciniscani emigrants began to return home and invest in the local economy. Eventually the population stabilized. War, particularly World War II, caused further serious economic hardship. But the town recovered and rebuilt and expanded. Today the town has a much smaller population and most industry is gone. Tourism, however, has come to play a very significant role in the economy. Festivals celebrating food, music, dance and literature are held in Picinisco, as well as religious celebrations. A significant amount of trade comes from Picinisco's proximity to the National Park. New restaurants and luxury accommodations have attracted others to the area. In addition, Picinisco is known world-wide as the center for the production of a variety of specialty meats and cheeses, as well as olive oil and liqueurs. All of this activity has caused a resurgence of the town's economic base.

Agriculture

For the Piciniscani, farming has never been a large-scale operation, primarily because the topography of the region offers limited flat space for growing. At the time of the earliest settlement in Picinisco every family would have had an "orta" - a kitchen garden to grow produce for the family's consumption - under the care of the women and children of the house. They also took care of all the domestic animals. Men and boys attended the marketable crops: grains, fruit orchards, olive groves and vineyards. From the town's founding, through to the twentieth century, more people were employed in the business of agriculture (by a very large margin) than in any other economic activity in Picinisco.

Crops were grown outside the walls of Picinisco, so farmers typically had to travel some distance to reach their fields, or establish their homes outside the town walls. Beyond the normal rigors of medieval farming, the forces of nature peculiar to the Comino Valley presented additional challenges: earthquakes, excessive rain and flooding, and fires created by thunderstorms ranging the hillsides. Farmers needed armed guards to protect their fields day and night from the many wild animals roaming the mountains and the gangs of brigands and thieves all too willing to steal produce.

Throughout the feudal period, farming involved a very high level of economic risk for the farmer. Assuming he did not own his own land (and most did not), the farmer had an obligation to pay for his use of the land with either a fixed amount or a percentage of his production. If it was a fixed amount, the farmer bore the entire risk of a bad harvest and he, and all of the members of his family, could suffer in debtor's prison for failing to produce enough to meet their rent. If payment was a portion of his harvest, the farmer may have avoided debtor's prison but may not have been able to feed his family in times of poor harvest. In the early 1800s, because of the confiscation of Church property and abolishment of feudal ownership, some farmers were able to become landowners. Then the farmer had an incentive to make improvements on his property as he alone would reap the economic benefit. Over the next several decades, as the population of Picinisco continued to expand, farmland became exhausted by continuous use and fields became less productive. Farms also grew smaller and smaller as the farmer divided his holdings among succeeding generations. By the end of the 1800s, many of those engaged in farming in Picinisco could no longer make a decent living and emigrated with their families. Today, only a fraction of farmland is actually under cultivation.

Grains. Grains were the first commodity produced in Picinisco for market (typically, farro, barley, rye and wheat). The crop demanded long, hard work which required the early farmer to be a jack-of-all trades. The fields had to be cleared of all rocks and trees, ditches had to be dug for water, the soil had to be fertilized, seeds had to be sewn, the crop weeded and eventually harvested. Initially, all of this had to be done by hand with the most rudimentary of hoes or plows, often made by the farmer himself. Eventually farmers used mules to haul plows and by the nineteenth century some oxen were employed in the effort. Harvesting required the work of the whole family and likely neighboring families as well. Grains were gathered to be threshed by hand or milled.

Grain was heavy and bulky to transport so whatever the farmer was able to keep after satisfying the landowner, he bartered or sold as locally as possible. Even in the small local markets, the farmer may have been at the mercy of the feudal landowner who could require the farmer to wait until the landowner disposed of all his grain before the farmer tried to sell anything. When there were price fluctuations, often a feudal landowner had grain storage facilities that would let him wait until prices rose again to sell. It was extremely difficult for the average peasant farmer to get ahead.

Olive Oil. Olive oil has always been an important commodity in Picinisco. Both the Church and the feudal lord owned olive orchards, as evidenced by inventories dating from the early 1500s. Olive trees had to be regularly pruned, grafted, and fertilized by hand. Harvesting olives required precise timing as well; olives picked too young would be sour and those picked too late would be without taste. Men on ladders carefully harvested the branches so as not to ruin the trees and women and children picked through what landed on the ground. It was a labor-intensive crop (more so than grapes), but there was a ready market locally as everyone used olive oil for cooking.

Olive oil became important to the textile industry as well. It was used to soften cloth and improve its quality. Terra di Lavoro, the province in which Picinisco was located, became the second largest exporter of olive oil in the Kingdom of Naples. Transportation issues may have prevented wide-ranging export of Picinisco olive oil during the middle ages. However, in the 1700s, a communal olive press was opened in Picinisco suggesting that larger quantities were being produced than previously was the case. Perhaps this was the reason that a soap factory opened in Picinisco in the mid 1800s. Olive oil soap was coveted all over Europe. As transportation improved, Picinisco's olive oil likely had a significantly wider distribution. Today, it is shipped all over the world.

Wine. Like olive oil, wine was undoubtedly made in Picinisco for personal consumption from the earliest days of the settlement. The vines required close attention during the growing season and the grapes had to be picked at just the right time to ensure the quality of the wine.   In the middle ages, Terra di Lavoro was the most important wine-producing region in the Kingdom of Naples and the biggest exporter of wine.   The wine made in the mountainous Picinisco region had a unique taste because the vines were typically planted among orchards of hazelnut, chestnut, fruits and olives. At the end of the 1500s, the white wine of Picinisco was described as "well-known as the best wine in the countryside". It is likely this wine was the ancient Maturano variety. Some of the feudal lord's share of the harvest traveled to markets beyond those in the Duchy of Alvito. Certainly today the harvest is enjoyed by a worldwide market and several older varieties of grapes are being actively cultivated.

Fruits. An abundance of fruit grows in Picinisco and some of the oldest varieties, like prugna pizzutelle (plums), are reemerging as specialty products in today's markets.   Apples, pears, cherries, pomegranates, persimmons and figs have been harvested in Picinisco for generations.   Eventually, as these fruits were preserved, dried fruit and jams from the region were enjoyed throughout the Kingdom of Naples.

Animal Husbandry

Sheepherding.   For many hundreds of years, the next most populous category of professions in Picinisco was animal husbandry - primarily sheepherding. Picinisco was particularly well situated for this type of economic activity given its proximity to some of the finest mountain summer pastures in the world - with rich and abundant varieties of plant life and pure mountain springs. Sheep were always an important commodity in southern Italy: their wool was used to produce cloth; their milk was used to produce cheese; and young lambs were sold for meat. In fact, throughout the middle ages, taxes on those engaged in animal husbandry were much higher than for those engaged in agriculture, in recognition of the profitability of animal husbandry.   In Picinisco, the principal sheepherding communities were located in in the frazioni at the highest elevation levels of the comune: Valleporcina and Fontitune.

The early shepherds of Picinisco were likely taking care of sheep owned by the feudal lord, the Church, or other wealthy individuals. A few farmers owned small numbers of sheep for the fertilizer they could provide and kept them as domesticated livestock. At the end of the summer these flocks had to be moved off the mountains near Picinisco to warmer, fertile plains for winter pasturage and for shearing near a large wool market. This seasonal movement of flocks was called the "transumanza" (or "transhumance"), which literally means "crossing the land." The practice of transumanza in Italy began in pre-Roman times and the first tax on herd movement was imposed by the Romans. The movement of vast numbers of sheep required cooperation from the owners of all the lands the shepherds had to cross, as well as a place for the flock to stay during the winter. Organized political support for this activity came after the Norman invasion in the middle of the thirteenth century, when the government established the Drogana delle Pecore (a custom house dealing with sheep) to tax and regulate seasonal flock movement and lease government-owned property for seasonal grazing. Though this first system fell apart as the political situation changed in the south of Italy, it was resurrected in the mid-1400s much more effectively.

In 1447, Alfonso I of Aragon passed a law called the "Regia Dogana della Mena delle Pecore di Puglia" creating a governmental administrative body to regulate the transumanza in southern Italy. Sheep owners were required to take their animals to spend the winter months on the southern plains of Puglia (called the "Tavogliere") and pay a tax for the "mena" or movement of the animals. The Dogana then regulated where the flocks would travel, the amounts landowners would be paid for sheep-grazing during the migration, ensured safe passage for migrating flocks, and took on the responsibility for adjudicating disputes. This regulated transumanza system ensured the crown in Naples could collect the maximum revenue from taxes and tolls on the very lucrative wool trade. Feudal nobles and the Church were able to arrange special concessions from the king, such as lower grazing fees and exemption from taxes on sales of wool, to favor their own larger flocks. Interestingly, however, many of those participating in the transumanza to Puglia were small herd owners. In a registry published by the Dogana for 1494/95, over 75% of the sheep-owners had less than 2000 sheep and 20% had flocks of 500 or fewer sheep. What is not well documented is how many sheep in the Kingdom of Naples were not part of this regular migration - they were known as the "sedentary sheep" population - at this point in history. Nor is there any specific data about flocks and shepherds of Picinisco.

The paths along which the animals were moved from the mountains to the plains were called "tratturi". These tratturi were fairly wide swatches of rich grasslands that were required to sustain the herds as they moved from summer to winter pastures. In 1549, the tratturi were the subject of new laws designed to regularize the system. The law identified three major tratturi and provided that each was to be maintained as a 110-meter-wide path that no one was permitted to block by farming or planting of trees or otherwise. These three tratturi were: the L'Aquila to Foggia track, the Castel di Sangro to Lucera track and the Pescasseroli to Candela track. In addition, the law provided that the "tratturelli", which were the main branches of paths leading to the tratturi, had to be maintained at 60 yards in width and the smaller "bracci", that connected the villages to the tratturelli, had to be maintained at 17 meters in width. The timing of the herd movement was also specifically regulated so that those in the valley could anticipate when the migrating sheep would arrive and sheriffs and militia located along the tratturi could provide protection to the shepherds and flocks.

The beginning of the tratturi were marked with white stones bearing the mark "RT" for "Regio Tratturi" or royal tracks. The flocks left the Picinisco area in late September or early October and took about 2 to 3 weeks to make the trip to Puglia. They typically returned in April or May. Along these tracks the shepherds could stop with their flocks at various "tratturali" - small structures designed to offer food, safe shelter and a place of worship for the travelers. There were pens to hold sheep for milking and stables for mules and pack horses. A real sharing of culture occurred as these travelers exchanged goods and information from the mountains to the plains.

A person could be employed in the transumanza in a variety of ways and the hierarchy of responsibility and earnings was very clearly defined and regulated. The head of the migrating group was called the "massero" or manager, usually the owner or the owner's representative, and he had control over all the participants in his group. The massero would have had an assistant (sotto-massero) and a dairyman (caciaro) responsible for milking and cheese production. The butteri were responsible for taking care of the mules and horses and other means of transport during the trip and for procuring firewood and resting places and transporting cheeses to market. The shepherds watched the flocks and the young boys on the trip (garzoni – as young as nine or ten) did whatever jobs might be assigned to them.

When the group arrived in Puglia they settled down for the winter months with their herds. Generally, they were located well outside any towns or cities and rarely interacted with the local people. They slept together on sheepskins in large huts and spent their days collecting milk, making cheese and grazing the herds. Typically, a shepherd was only allowed a pass to travel home once a month. In the spring before the flocks could return home, the sheep had to be washed, shorn and the wool sold at market. Washing the sheep involved complicated maneuvering of flocks through fast-running streams several times for the cleanest wool. Apparently the buyers in the market in Foggia thought the finest wool had been washed in this manner a minimum of three times before the sheep were shorn. With smaller herds, the shepherds would shear the sheep themselves, although the plains of Puglia were full of master shearers who came to ply their trade. Once the wool was sold at the large wool market in Foggia the group could return home to the mountains for the summer and reunite with their families. Often they traveled at night to avoid the heat. It was slow going as there were many new lambs and the sheep had to be milked twice a day.

Fortunately for the Piciniscani, during the summer months their homes were closest to the finest mountain pastures in the region. When the shepherds arrived back from the winter they would herd their flocks right through the center of town and stop for a blessing from the priest. Shepherds from Picinisco followed the same trails up into the mountains and used the same pastures year in and year out so they could always be located by their families and could return home to help with farming and other domestic animals.

The shepherds of Picinisco carried whatever supplies they needed: a knife, a gourd for water and maybe another for olive oil, a bullock's horn filled with salt, a copper pot, a sack of unshelled corn and two flat stones for grinding it, tobacco rolled into the shape of a sausage and tied tightly, slingshots to go after smaller predators, and nets made of hemp that they used to pen the sheep. They also carried umbrellas fashioned from sticks and iron with a covering often decorated with solar symbols and a handle that might be carved in the shape of an animal. These umbrellas provided protection as well as a walking stick and prod for the sheep. During the time up on the mountain, the Piciniscani shepherds stayed in crude dry-stone huts, which were often destroyed during the winter months and had to be rebuilt. Sometimes their only shelter was in a cave or underneath an outcropping of rocks. Most of their meals consisted of sheep-milk and polenta mixed with water and boiled in a pot. Occasionally the shepherds shaped the polenta into patties they would brown over a slow fire.

Most importantly, the shepherds were accompanied by their dogs, who served as both companions and defenders up in the mountains. Long ago, shepherds used mastiff sheepdogs; they were large, white animals weighing in at 65 to 110 pounds and 23 to 29 inches tall. Each dog wore a collar with pointed spikes sharp enough to fight off wolves, bears and other wild animals that might threaten the herds. It is said that two of these dogs were capable of killing a wolf. Their collars were made of wood and decorated by the Piciniscani shepherds to show the ownership of the animal. Because the sheepdogs were white in color they could easily hide among the sheep and then surprise an attacker by jumping out from the herd. These huge sheepdogs were also employed to help the men repel attacks by brigands and other criminal elements taking refuge in the mountains. Piciniscani shepherds were particularly known for the complicated whistles they employed to signal their animals to turn or stop the herd.

As the men and boys watched their herds they were never completely idle: there was milking to be done twice daily and cheese to be made and transported to market. During periods of rest they would carve wooden collars for their sheep and dogs with intricate patterns, play musical instruments, and sing in harmony with other shepherds on the mountain. Younger shepherds would carve all manner of household items (spoons, forks, spindles for a loom, broom handles) and decorate them with flowers or animals for young women they hoped to court in town. Living mostly alone and only by their wits, these men were sharp-sighted and quick of hearing. They could tell the exact hour of the day according to the shadow of the sun and could travel at night following the stars as well as any ancient mariner. Shepherds were thought to possess great wisdom and patience. They used their imaginations to pass long solitary times inventing songs, telling tales and reciting poetry and were in constant communication with God and the saints.

The long-range, cross-regional transumanza (which came to be known as the "horizontal" transumanza) lasted until the early 1800s. Napoleon closed the Dogana in an effort to promote cultivation of land for agricultural purposes rather than grazing. Thereafter, the transumanza had to be organized on a piecemeal basis, with no protections offered in terms of safety or prices for use of the land.

This is when shepherds turned to a short-range or "vertical" transumanza - moving their flocks from the mountains to a closer field to pass the winter months. Many Piciniscani shepherds chose to winter in Caserta near the sea and along the way they stayed with families who consented to host them to keep the costs down.

The market for meat, milk and cheese during the months the shepherds were in Picinisco was basically local, but the Piciniscani shepherds were always known throughout the Duchy for their fine cheeses and likely served the entire Comino Valley and beyond. Early in the 1800s, the family Bartolomucci established a large dairy operation in Picinisco capable of distributing products to larger markets much farther away. They maintained a herd of cattle as well, though cattle were not in abundance in Picinisco. Sheepherding continued to be a vital industry in Picinisco following the Napoleonic reforms. The fame of the Picinisco pecorino and ricotta cheeses eventually spread throughout the world. Although the number of shepherd families in Picinisco has declined steadily in the last century, the industry is still a large part of the identity of Picinisco: the town's largest annual festival, drawing thousands of visitors, is the "Pastorizia in Festival" celebrating the industry and its heritage in August.

Pigs. Pigs were also important to the economy of the region. In and around Picinisco, pigs were most often bred and grazed in a semi-wild state in the bountiful forests. For families of peasants, a single pig could make a huge difference to their food stores, as sausage, bacon and prosciutto would be prepared and stored for later consumption. A family fortunate enough to find several pigs could sell the meat at local markets. Some families specialized in the breeding of pigs, others in caring for herds of pigs owned by the nobility. Pigs were an important commodity and their grazing and theft were frequent subjects of concern in the community. In the middle ages, a pig or shoulder of pork was the required form of annual contribution by Piciniscani churches to the Bishop in Sora.

Pigs were classified in terms of color: white, red and black. For the wealthy, white was believed to have no culinary appeal, red was considered "tasty," but it was the black pig that was highly valued. This black pig was known as the Casertano Maiale Nero (a "Black Pig" originating in nearby Caserta), an ancient breed coveted for its superior quality of meat since early Roman times. The pig was characterized by its dark color (purple/black or slate gray), lack of bristles, and glands growing behind its cheek, and was believed to be quite resistant to disease.   It was particularly suited to the topography of Picinisco as a semi-wild breed, living off of acorns, chestnuts, walnuts and wild fruits - all of which are in abundance in the area.   When fully fattened for slaughter, between 12 and 24 months, these pigs could be over 400 pounds in weight. The breed began to decline during the food shortages caused by World War II, and was almost obliterated by the introduction an inferior breed of white pig to the area that cross-bred with the Maiale Nero in the 1960s. Today pig farmers, including several in the Picinisco area, are working to revive the breed and to secure the coveted DOP rating for their prized meat products.

Other Livestock. Piciniscani residents found work with other types of animals as well. Some worked in transportation, taking care of mules and a small number of horses. A limited number of cattle were grazed in Picinisco, primarily for their beef, and some residents were employed in their care.   Goats were often maintained by the shepherds as part of the herds of sheep and their milk was used in the production of cheese, although goats were not as profitable as sheep. Still today, the DOC Pecorino Cheese of Picinisco is prepared with goat's milk from the breeds known as capra grigia ciociara and capra bianca monticellana found in and around Picinisco.   The Piciniscani also maintained rabbits and chickens for market locally and eventually beyond.

Millwork

Mills have been in operation in Picinisco since the first settlement, in the eleventh century. Picinisco's "Mole di Vito," which dates from 1613, has been continuously in use since then, even to this day. The earliest mills were grinding grains and nuts using a rudimentary mill stone operated by hydraulic power from the rivers. Next to develop were mills used in the textile industry. These mills were for "fulling," a process which worked wool and hemp cloth to clean it and to thicken it to a felt-like material. As the formerly urban textile industry of southern Italy began moving to the countryside, this type of mill became even more lucrative. Finally, by the nineteenth century, a paper mill operating in Picinisco produced paper prized all over Europe.

Although the earliest millers in Picinisco likely owned their land and built their own mills, they could only operate the mill with a license from the feudal lord, who had exclusive control over the waterways in Picinisco. Typically, the feudal lord took a portion of whatever was being milled as payment for this license to operate. In 1595, for example, the feudal lord's share was 2/3 of the mill's output. The feudal lord also had the right to mandate the use of a particular mill by other towns in his duchy. When the Gallio family first took over the Duchy of Alvito, the Picinisco grain mills had to be used by citizens of the nearby towns of San Donato and Settefrati, and the Picinisco fulling mill had to be used by everyone in the Duchy. By the time Francesco Gallio became the feudal lord in the 1600s, he recognized the economic potential of the mills and conceived of a plan to increase his earnings by purchasing all of the mills on the Melfa River outright.

Perhaps the most profitable of all the mills was the paper mill developed by the Bartolomucci family in the early 1800s. The mill, located in the frazione of Borgo Castellone, was actually originally founded by the same Francesco Gallio in the 1600s. But it was the Bartolomucci family who was responsible for its conversion to a paper mill that eventually supplied over twenty types of the highest quality of paper. Among its purchasers was the government of the Kingdom of Naples. At the beginning of the 1800s, the Bartolomuccis employed over 60 men and women in their paper operation and their success enabled them to build an extensive complex of buildings, including housing for employees. By the end of the 1800s, they employed almost 100 men and women and owned a warehouse in Naples for storage. A wealthy mill-owner from Atina, Visocchi, acquired a partial interest in the mill and eventually, at the turn of the century, the Bartolomuccis sold their entire interest to him. The mill did not survive the modernization of the paper industry in the 1900s. Today the mill has been transformed into a beautiful community of private apartments.

Textile Industry

With sheep and the fulling mills located in Picinisco, it is hardly surprising that a small textile industry ultimately developed there. Picinisco also had a ready supply of saffron and other plants used to produce textile dyes on its nearby mountainside. People were employed as wool carders, spinners, and weavers, and wool, linen and hemp were sold in nearby markets by the 1600s. By the 1700s, small cottage industries were created by women who made beautiful bedcovers and carpets woven on home looms with patterns that became known throughout the Kingdom. Other women specialized in embroidery and made lace sold all over the kingdom. Even into the 1800s, there were a significant number of individuals employed in the textile industry, suggesting production went well beyond the needs of the Piciniscani and likely supplied textiles to a much broader market. In fact, cloth made in Picinisco was used for uniforms for the army of the Kingdom of Naples and later for the alpine soldiers of the Italian national army. A British gazette, dated in 1855, identifies Picinisco by reference to only one industry - the manufacture of "woolen covers". Today the textile industry is largely gone from Picinisco, but there are isolated crafters still pursuing these bygone arts.

Mining

From the time of the Roman Empire, it was known that minerals existed in the mountains near Picinisco. Iron useful to early military needs was abundant. Gold had been seen in the riverbed of the Melfa River near Picinisco. There was also alabaster in caves in the mountains and reports of silver found in mountain streams. However, the difficulty of transportation made large-scale mining unprofitable.

The first recorded mineral exploitation in Picinisco by the crown in Naples dates from the late 1700s when the King decided to begin mining operations there on a large scale. With the hydraulic power of the River Melfa and the ready supply of fuel from the surrounding forests, Picinisco was a perfect location for a large foundry and many men and machines were brought in to work in this mining operation. They mined for iron, magnesium and asphalt. Ultimately pricing issues and the problems of transportation caused the mining operation to be abandoned early in the 1800s. The King of Naples determined to undertake a new exploitation project in the mid-1800s and the same mines were reopened for production. However, this later project did not result in the expected returns and no large-scale mining was ever accomplished again.

Forestry

Surrounding Picinisco there are forests filled with beech, oak, chestnut and walnut trees, as well as some pine, ash and other varieties. The woods were a source of fuel for everyone and a source of raw material for the earliest craftsmen and for the construction and furniture trades. People living near the edge of the forests were experts in fashioning bows and arrows. At the beginning of the 1800s, those identified as "carpenters" number the second largest group of tradesmen after farming. The forests fueled the mining industry and also supplied the raw material for those who made charcoal used for cooking and heating.

Since the woods were part of the "common lands" for hundreds of years, anyone could access them for a fee and common use dictated some reforestation effort on the part of the user. After Napoleon eliminated the law of the "common lands" in the early 1800s, private owners had no obligation to reforest. Their extensive clear-cutting for commercial exploitation jeopardized the continued use of the forests. It was partially in recognition of the problems of extensive deforestation in the early 1900s that the National Park on Picinisco's border was created and forestry became heavily regulated in the area.

Professionals

The first professionals in Picinisco were the judge and a notary who participated in a conveyance of property by the Marsi family. Generally, a notary was responsible for recording a document and a judge was responsible for the legality of the conveyance. In both cases the individuals had to be trained and be able to read and write to engage in such professions. By the late 1500s, Picinisco's population included doctors of law and medicine, as well as a surgeon. All of these professionals had to receive at least some kind of training, a luxury likely available only to the very wealthy or someone who could secure a patron among the nobility or religious order.

Other professionals were involved with the management of the feudal estate or town government. The "bagliva" of Picinisco was a bailiff responsible for enforcing laws, dealing with nonviolent crimes and small civil lawsuits and for maintaining a jail.   Picinisco's "portolania" was responsible for the maintenance of streets, construction of wells and sewers, and levying fines for infractions. The office of the "zecca" was held by a person who established the system of weights and measures and enforced compliance with certain standards.   The "camelegna" was the treasurer or accountant of Picinisco who oversaw all the tax collections.   The "Mastro Massaro" was an agriculture specialist in charge of the feudal lord's agricultural properties.   Eventually there were teachers hired to educate the children of Picinisco.   Collectively, however, these professionals represented a very small minority of the total population of Picinisco - well into the twentieth century.

Skilled Trades

A survey of professions reported by the Piciniscani around 1810 indicates there were a wide variety of skilled tradesmen in the town. In the construction industry, there were those who quarried stone and fashioned wrought-iron, as well as carpenters.   There were men who worked transporting goods.   Several butchers and blacksmiths had establishments in town to attend the animals. There were also cobblers and tailors.   Some musicians made their living playing the zampogna (a special kind of bagpipe).   At least one midwife served the female population of Picinisco in the 1800s. A number of people listed their vocation as shopkeepers.   A few were part of a military force.   And there were many priests who lived in and served the community.

Women

Women worked alongside men who farmed for their livings.   Many also worked in the textile industry, as well as individual cottage industries in lacemaking and weaving.   Women also found employment providing domestic services to the church and the bourgeoisie class.   They cooked and cleaned and provided laundry services.   Laundry was a complicated process requiring the gathering of firewood, boiling cauldrons of water, washing at communal washing posts or streams with soap made at home, spreading the laundry to dry on trees and stones, and ironing with heavy irons heated in the fire. Knitting, sewing and mending were also taken on by women for extra income. Many of their own household chores could be expanded to increase the family revenue: women produced extra candles, baked extra loaves of bread, and preserved extra fruit for sale. Women were employed in the production of baskets, particularly those used by shepherds who made the special cheeses of Picinisco. Interestingly, in records maintained by the community at the beginning of the 1800s, every woman is identified by her own individual profession, beyond that of a wife and mother.

Seasonal Economic Opportunities

There were also economic opportunities that came to the community on a seasonal basis. Foraging in the mountains and forests at various times of the year could augment a family's food stores and possibly their profits as well. Mushrooms, especially truffles, were prized at market. Many medicinal plants used by apothecaries in Naples grew in the mountains and forests of Picinisco, as well as plants used in dyeing cloth for the textile industry. The woods were also filled with acorns, walnuts and chestnuts that could be gathered and sold. Honey could be collected from beehives and wild fruits and vegetables, like asparagus, picked from mountainside slopes. The Piciniscani trained falcons to assist hunting parties which were very popular by the 1600s. They hunted red and roe deer, chamois, mountain hare, wild boar and hedgehogs that were plentiful in the mountains. Hunting continued in the area until the beginning of the 1900s when the National Park was established. Ice could be gathered from the mountaintop for transport to market. By the mid-1800s, as more people traveled to southern Italy from Europe and Great Britain, Mt. Meta became a fascination with alpine climbers. They found guides among the Piciniscani to take them to the top, a 12-hour walk from the town center. Both British and Italian alpine guidebooks recommended Picinisco as the best place to spend the night and acquire the very best mountain guides.

Chapter 8

Society and Class

From the start, Picinisco's population was divided into several social strata. There is an old saying that southern Italian society can be divided among "those who fight, those who pray and those who work" meaning the nobility, the clergy and the peasants. That is perhaps a bit too simplistic an analysis. The 1054AD land transfer that first mentions Picinisco indicates the presence of a noble family in control of land (the Marsi family), the Abbey of Montecassino, the professionals, a judge and notary, who drew up the papers for the land transfer, and two citizens of the town who witnessed the transfer, neither of whom could read or write. At the top of the social pyramid were the nobles and then the clergy. Their power was derived from wealth and military strength and the importance of religion to the community. Below them, but considered above the peasantry, were those trained in a profession, particularly a notary or judge. The fact of their training implied the existence of some level of wealth, since education was a luxury and not available to everyone. The witnesses to the land transfer, like virtually everyone else in Picinisco, belonged to the lowest level of society: laborers who worked land that belonged to the nobles or the Church.

This societal division began to shift sometime around the middle of the millennium. The feudal lord and the clergy remained at the top of the social strata. However, a definite middle class of quasi-bourgeoisie began to emerge. This class still included the professionals, including lawyers, doctors and surgeons. Joining the professionals were the few people in Picinisco who were able to buy land or secure lucrative leases that allowed them to hire others to work their land. Also in this class were individuals who held official positions granted to them by the feudal lord or the Università. The skilled tradesmen who had some economic independence were also differentiated from the peasants. Still, the largest and the lowest level of society included those who had no property of their own and relied on others for employment. Day laborers, servants, sheepherders, and sharecroppers populated this class. We know from church records that there was also a class of paupers who lived in Picinisco whom the community supported.

A person's place in society was clear to everyone in the town and proper respect was shown by those of lower classes to their superiors. The first recorded visit of a feudal lord to Picinisco was Cardinal Gallio in 1595, and he was revered and feted by the Piciniscani. Later Gallio family dukes visited Picinisco to participate in religious celebrations or to hunt and fish, but never to conduct business or simply visit.   The Duke was above participation in everyday life; he was the ruler and protector of the community and he employed others to attend to his property.   The Gallio dukes cultivated a "nobless oblige" persona, ensuring public ceremony for their benevolent contributions to the poor or orphaned or donations to the church or schools.   The Gallio's castle in Picinisco stood as an everyday testament to their wealth and power.

The respect accorded to the clergy, second only to the feudal lord, was due to the importance placed on religion by the people of Picinisco, but also because the Church was extremely wealthy and extremely powerful, even in this small community.   It was the second largest property owner in Picinisco; besides its many church buildings, the Church owned orchards, vineyards and farm properties.   The priests dressed in elaborate robes on special occasions and their churches were filled with gold and silver ornamentation. The Church could provide money to those in need through outright welfare or by lending money, at times even lending to the Università. Every written description of the most prominent people of Picinisco (well into the nineteenth century) has included the names of all of the priests and abbots in the town. Interestingly, most of them came from the families of the Piciniscani; even the lowest peasant could increase his status in the community by having his son become a priest.

In the 1700 and 1800s, a small minority of the Piciniscani joined the class of rural bourgeoisie as they acquired land or shops in the town. They emulated the feudal lord by building larger, more ornate homes and becoming patrons of the Church. They socialized only with those of their class and arranged marriages among themselves. In fact, well into the 1800s, marriages were arranged between families engaged in the exact same occupations - landowner to landowner, shopkeeper to shopkeeper and shepherd to shepherd.   The abolishment of feudal ownership and the confiscation of church property in the early 1800s were meant to change the social order by providing peasants with the opportunity to acquire land.   However, neither the feudal lord nor the clergy suffered an immediate drop in social status. The feudal lord still owned significant property and spent years in court haggling over the ownership of the rest. The Church suffered, but it's prestige in the community was based as much on its status as a religious leader, which continued uninterrupted. The rural bourgeoisie were able to acquire more land and positions of political prominence in this changed situation, but the lower class of peasantry did not have enough money to change their status significantly.

The hierarchy of these social strata continued even after Italy was unified in 1861. But change was inevitable. In the new Italian state, political leadership began to emerge as a factor in social status. Economic success through land ownership, crucial to social standing, became more accessible as emigrants sent money back to Picinisco or returned themselves to purchase properties. More money meant more educational opportunities for those in the peasant class to train as professionals, thus elevating their positions. Women entered the workforce in large numbers and gradually achieved a level of equality that changed their status in the community. The separation of church and state diminished the Catholic Church's political power, but in Picinisco the Church and its clergy are still held in high esteem and accorded the respect and reverence of years gone by.

Chapter 9

Personal Characteristics & Traditional Dress

From paintings and older photographs, we can see that many of the people of Picinisco were quite attractive, particularly as depicted in their unusual and colorful traditional dress. Both men and women had classical facial features, dark eyes and luxuriant dark hair. They were fairly small in stature, but extremely muscular in appearance. Their isolated living situation meant the bloodlines of the families were rarely crossed by outsiders for the first several hundred years. Such isolation, and the abundant natural resources that surrounded Picinisco, may account for the fact that many lived long and healthy lives. In terms of personality, the Piciniscani were very friendly towards their infrequent visitors, but tended to be very private and fiercely protective of their own. The family was the center to be safeguarded and defended at all costs.

Longevity. A variety of factors could account for the longevity of the lives of the Piciniscani. To begin with: diet. For hundreds of years the Piciniscani ate meat only very rarely, instead consuming a diet rich in fresh vegetables, herbs, nuts, fruits and grains, and water from fresh mountain streams. The Fonte Scopella, the oldest communal fountain in Picinisco, is thought, even now, to have properties that cure disease. Secondly, Picinisco's isolated mountain location protected the population from the many diseases that plagued urban European communities in the middle ages. Thirdly, the population had plenty of exercise from morning until night with farming, shepherding, and household chores. Everyone walked, everywhere (animals were used to transport goods, not people, well into the twentieth century). Even the elderly residents of town walked up and down the mountain to church, often on a daily basis. One might also attribute the longevity of the Piciniscani to the beauty and serenity of their natural surroundings. While there was certainly stress in their daily lives, they couldn't help but be affected by the natural beauty visible all around them. Whatever the cause, the Abbot de Antiquis, writing in 1622, said that the Piciniscani often attained the "reputable age of 120 with sight so perfect that they could easily insert thread in a needle, albeit without teeth to eat crusts of bread."

While a long life was not unusual for the men of Picinisco, the same statistic is not necessarily true for women and children, particularly until Italian unification brought more universal healthcare to the region. The early death of women of child-bearing age was not uncommon. Women married young and bore children often, as the Catholic Church did not sanction birth control. It was not unusual to have a baby born at least every two years and many women had more than eight pregnancies during their lifetimes. These same women were responsible for taking care of their households, their children, their gardens their livestock and their fields. Whether because of work or the risks of childbirth, they often died at a young age. However, those women who did survive were very tough, as witnessed by travelers to the area who frequently commented on their ferocity. Most women in Picinisco knew how to use a knife and a gun to protect themselves and their families. They developed tremendous strength carrying heavy loads of firewood and water up and down the mountain, typically on top of their heads. They had an abundance of courage, often facing life on their own as their men were away from home working.

Until the twentieth century it was generally accepted that many small children of Picinisco would not grow to adulthood. (Even in the early 1800s, almost half of the deaths registered in Picinisco were children under the age of 15). There were so many perils for young children of peasant farmers. Babies and young children often had to be left unattended or in the care of other children. Food contamination was prevalent due to lack of effective preservatives. Periods of malnutrition were particularly hard for youngsters to survive. Their accidental death was commonplace.

Personality. There are historical descriptions of the personality of the peasants of Picinisco, beginning as early as the 1500s. They are described as a cheerful, simple folk who accepted their lot in life and took joy in their beautiful surroundings. They were very hardworking and industrious; there are descriptions of women walking home behind a donkey laden with freshly harvested food and knitting all the while. Others have described the Piciniscani as being very private people, reluctant to involve themselves in the problems of others or the larger community. As a result, cooperation was sometimes difficult to achieve in the community. Although one-time visitors found the Piciniscani very friendly and curious about the outside world, those closer to the community surmise that the townspeople were more likely to be friendly to visitors whom they would never see again than to their neighbors who might keep track of favors.

"La bella figura" was also important to the Piciniscani (a concept referring not just to physical beauty, but to manners and behavior). They were neat in appearance (though before indoor plumbing, bathing was a once-a-week occurrence at best) and kept a set of their very best clothes for feast days. They had beautiful manners and were very respectful in their treatment of others. They would bow and kiss the hand of a woman in greeting and men would kiss one another on both cheeks. They referred to one another as "Don" or "Donna" as a sign of respect. Respect was important to the community; people knew their place in society and strictly observed social mores. The Piciniscani had no desire to rebel against this social order, believing that reaching for more than what they had could be futile, if not dangerous.

Loyalty to family was of the utmost importance to the Piciniscani. Each member of the family was expected to support any decision made by the male head of the household and to defend those decisions within the community. Feuds between families could last for generations, preventing marriages and property transactions and even inciting violence. An offense against one family member was an offense against all members of the family. Family loyalty was strictly enforced; anyone who broke this bond was considered an outcast.

The Piciniscani were very religious and at the same time very superstitious. Community values were strongly aligned with the teachings of the Catholic Church and any break with what was "proper" Catholic behavior was universally condemned. They attended mass regularly and asked the local priests to bless their animals and crops, as well as their families. They would keep a religious talisman on their person and in their houses and build shrines in the mountains to ensure they had a place to worship. However, this did not mean the Piciniscani followed the dictates of Catholicism blindly. A favorite proverb of the Piciniscani translates as follows: "if you do the same bad thing to someone else that they did to you, it is not a sin." Nor did the Piciniscani leave good fortune to chance; they believed in the benefit of an amulet to ward off evil spirits. The entire community respected the power of the "malocchio" (the evil eye).

Traditional Dress.   One of the most unique features of the traditional attire of the peasants of the Comino Valley is their footwear.   The "ciocia" (the plural form is "ciocie") sandals are peculiar to those who live in the mountains of southern Lazio and nearby Abruzzo and Molise and over time have come to define an area and a way of living known as "Ciociaria".   These sandals are particularly well-suited to the region, providing a sturdy foot-covering that is flexible enough to permit easy movement among the sometimes treacherous mountain slopes.

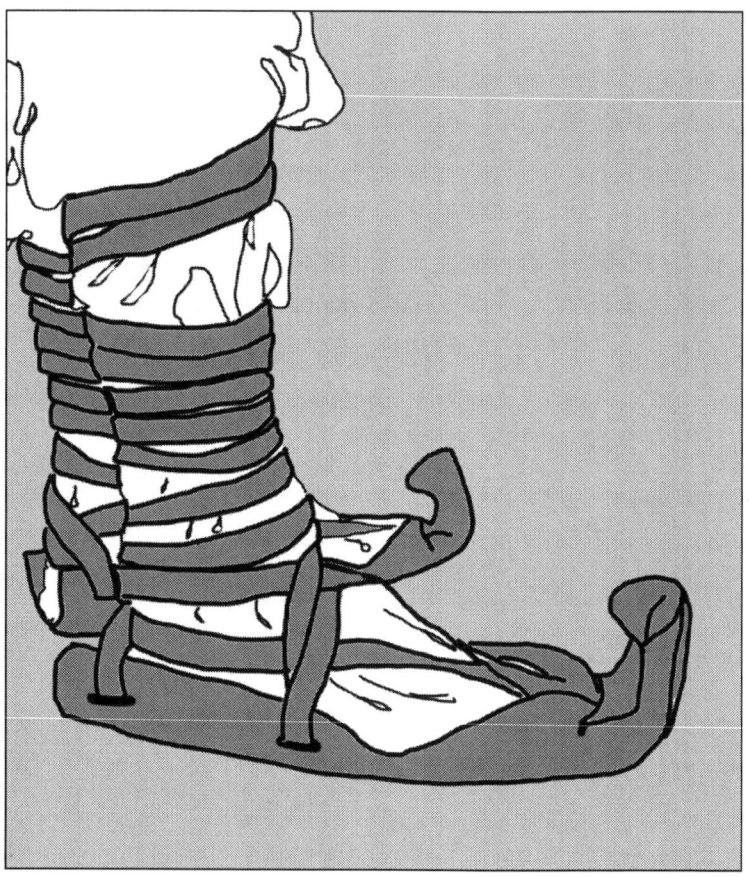

The ciocie were made from pieces of animal skin that were tanned and formed into the flat sole of the sandal.   The toe typically curled into a pointed tip.   There were holes around the outside edges of the sole through which were threaded long cords that were then crossed and re-crossed up the calf of the wearer. Shepherds wore a slightly larger version of this footwear, where the animal skin with the hair in place extended up the leg, causing them to look like the satyrs of ancient time. These sandals were worn in summer and in winter with the laces crossed over thick woolen stockings. They were the regular footwear of the Piciniscani right into the twentieth century.

Women. The traditional feast-day dress of the women of Picinisco was quite ornate. However, no undergarments were worn as they were impractical due to the lack of plumbing. They wore white blouses with huge billowing sleeves, stiffly starched, and beautifully embroidered collars and cuffs. Brightly colored skirts or dresses in green, lavender, or dark red, lavishly pleated, sometimes in velvet or silk, fell to just above the ankle, often flaring out because of multiple petticoats. Artists were particularly taken with the brilliant and subtle shades of color these women were able to achieve from natural plant dyes.

Over the skirt and blouse, or dress, there was a brightly colored, embroidered corset. On top of all of this, a scarf or shawl, decorated with fringe, sometimes white and sometimes brightly colored, hung around their necks and then crossed over their chests and tucked into the top of their skirts. Generally, their hair was piled on top of their heads, sometimes in braids, and pinned up with an ornate piece of jewelry (or occasionally a dagger!). On their heads, they wore what looked like large white handkerchiefs (the size of a hand towel), usually elaborately folded in the front, and continuing down the back, held together there with a broach.

For everyday wear, blouses and skirts were made of coarser, plainer fabric and the white blouse was not decorated (but still had large billowing sleeves). The shawl was less elaborate and typically tucked into a large apron. Hair was still done up and the large white fabric (of a lesser quality) draped on their heads. Jewelry worn everyday was typically large gold hoop earrings, sometimes with a hanging moon or star shape. Necklaces of gold and coral, gold bangles and rings might be worn on special occasions. In church, a woman would cover her head with an additional red or black cloth.

Men. The traditional dress of the men of Picinisco was not much different whether it was every day or a feast day. They wore black pants ending just below the knee topped by a white shirt and a red or blue vest and a short dark jacket. They wore scarves around their necks and a dark colored, alpine hat with a feather or flower in the brim. In the winter, a long cape was used over the vest or a shorter jacket with some sheepskin lining. A man from Picinisco typically wore his hat indoors and out.

Shepherds moving their flocks in the mountains had capes and coats made from sheepskin and often wore sheepskin chaps over their pants to keep warm. Looking at photographs of shepherds in the nineteenth century one can see how a shepherd could be lost from view as he wandered along with his flock since his clothing left

him covered almost head to foot in sheepskin! The shepherds carried a sort of purse to carry young sheep born during the journey and a saddlebag for their personal belongings.

Children. Children dressed essentially the same as adults.

Chapter 10

Daily Life

Early on, daily life was consumed with the effort to keep family fed and secure. For the men, this meant raising crops and animals and defending the community and their homes against attack by man and beast. For the women, this meant caring for children, the garden, and for everything associated with the home, as well as helping in the fields when necessary. But it would be impossible to live in a place as beautiful as Picinisco without taking in the natural wonders of the area on a daily basis. All around them were the often snow-capped peaks of the mountains, green hillsides, deep, dark forests, rivers of the most delicious clear and cold water, and the beautiful fertile valley of Comino below them.

There is virtually no information available about the daily lives of the Piciniscani at the time of its settlement in the eleventh century. Most descriptions have to do with the state of the land, not the people. A clearer picture emerges early in the 1800s and, given that change only occurred fairly slowly in Picinisco, may represent the best description of habitual activities of earlier years.

Every morning, the people of Picinisco would awaken early, have a simple breakfast of bread and fruit, and begin work. People were aware of the time passing during the day with reference to the sun or, within earshot of the village, by reference to the church bells that chimed the hour. (Even today the sounds of the Angelus can still be heard at 10 o'clock from the Church of Santa Maria Assunta). At noon, a large canon was fired in town to alert everyone, even those in the fields, that it was time to break for a meal. For most people, lunch was a light meal transported by women to wherever the men were working. Dinner was usually whatever was left over from lunch transformed into a hot meal at home.

Women in the town of Picinisco saw their neighbors often throughout the day as they gathered water from communal fountains, washed their clothes together at a communal washhouse and baked their bread together at communal ovens. Beginning in the 1800s, children met one another at school, but by the age of 8 or 9 had begun working in the fields or with the animals, and by 11 years of age, they worked an entire day as adults. When they were not at school or working in the fields children might congregate in the piazza or in the narrow streets of town and plays games with one another. Men out in the fields were fairly isolated and those working as shepherds might encounter one another on the mountains with their flocks or pass the night together there. People working in shops saw one another more often. People from outlying hamlets had a much smaller world, but met up with one another in the town of Picinisco to do business or at the municipal building or gathering their mail at the post office.

In the evening, when work was done, there was the "passeggiata" when people would stroll through the piazza and enjoy the view of the valley, stopping to have a drink or chat with their neighbors. Young people chaperoned by their parents might get a glimpse of one another. Men gathered to discuss politics or play a game of cards. They might also congregate at the bocce court below the piazza for a game. It was usually an early bedtime as work awaited everyone with the sunrise.

Sunday mass was a time when those in town and those living on outlying farms came together. The church bells would sound calling everyone into town. Those same church bells were used to gather the townspeople for announcements, elections, or when men were needed to defend the community.   There were many religious holidays throughout the year that the community celebrated together - often by attending mass followed by a communal meal in the piazza with singing and dancing. By 1889 Picinisco had its own town band.   Spring planting and the fall harvest brought the community together to help one another and were celebrated with community dinners and music and dancing.   There was a local market in Picinisco every Sunday for the members of the town and surrounding farms. Traveling peddlers brought goods produced in nearby cities to trade for the highly prized Picinisco pecorino or ricotta cheese or fruits and other local products. Small stands would be set up in the piazza and local produce traded.

Chapter 11

Dwellings

Many homes in today's Picinisco were constructed hundreds of years ago, some many hundreds of years ago. Of course over such a long period they have been damaged, due to natural disasters (earthquakes) and manmade disasters (bombing during World War II), and renovated for modern conveniences (indoor plumbing and electricity). Still, after 1000 years of history, it is possible to reconstruct what many of the earliest dwellings were like from a look inside the homes that remain today in this charming mountaintop village.

Homes of the Peasants. From the outside, the oldest peasant dwellings appeared to be solid and well-constructed; they were typically built of stone with walls as thick as 18 inches or more. This was a dry-stone construction. In the last several hundred years, the stone on the exterior walls of these homes has been covered with a smother, limestone (perhaps mixed with concrete) coating. Roofs from many hundreds of years ago were covered with curved terra cotta tiles and much earlier may have been covered with thatch or sod-like materials. Doors were typically cut as square entryways, wide enough for access for animals, carts and the like. Windows were almost nonexistent - typically one window, relatively small, was cut into the very thick stone walls of the house, and occasionally covered by iron bars or a shutter embedded into the wall.

The area just outside the house (if not within the town walls), including the family's garden, their woodpile, their well or cistern for catching rain water, and perhaps an enclosure for their pig, was often encircled by a dry-stone fence. As peasants prospered they might build a separate barn for domestic animals, possibly divided into stalls and storage areas, that would be enclosed within the dry-stone walls as well. These peasant homes were strictly utilitarian in appearance; late in the eighteenth century, when some residents began to enjoy a bit of prosperity, they added keystones atop their arched doorways with the family crest or other special identifying symbols. A balcony or special gate, fashioned in wrought-iron, might also have been added to the outside decor.

The interior of the house was very dark, almost cave-like, with its single window and door offering the only outside light in the home's single room. The ceiling was typically open with the wood framing exposed. Neither the walls nor the ceiling were weather-resistant and rain and snow easily penetrated the inside. The walls were dark with accumulations of smoke from the fire in the very large open hearth that dominated the room. The floor was laid with stone pebbles from nearby mountain streams or hard, beaten-down earth.

The main room served as a kitchen, barn and storage area, as well as a bedroom, unless a loft was built below the ceiling. The large open hearth provided heat and a place for cooking. Immediately next to the hearth was a huge basket filled with twigs, prunings from the orchards, olive pits, and chopped wood for the fire and a giant pair of bellows to keep the fire alive. Away from the fire, part of the room was given over to the storage of farming equipment and supplies - anything of value to the family's economic welfare. Netting tacked to the wall held the fodder for the animals, and a trough for feeding and watering was built along one of the walls.

The family's livestock were brought inside for the cold season, as well as for protection from theft by brigands. Mules, cows, oxen, chickens, dogs - even a pig - often shared the interior of the peasant's home, especially in the winter.

There was no running water in these homes until late in the twentieth century. Peasants dug wells and built huge cisterns to collect rain or, if they were close enough to a river or stream they could transport water from there. Transporting water was a job for women who carried large pots called "concone" on their heads. In this manner they supplied water for drinking, cooking, watering animals, and bathing. Bathing was done in a large copper tub filled with water heated over the fire. The effort required was too great to promote frequent bathing. No bathrooms existed inside of the house until well into the twentieth century. Most farm families used the manure pile or the field and kept a pot near the bed for nighttime visits. Much later, outhouses were built near the house and eventually indoor plumbing was available, though universal acceptance took some time.

For many hundreds of years there were meager furnishings in these dwellings and little or no decoration, except perhaps for some religious art. The portion of the room not taken over by animals or for storage was typically occupied by a table and chairs with straw seats or benches. Apart from the kitchen equipment there may have been a chest or cabinet to hold dishes. The family slept on mattresses stuffed with hay, corn husks or rags and if there was a bed frame it was constructed of wood and rope. Mattresses were shared by as many people as possible, often lined up head to foot. A woman's dowry chest might sit next to the bed for clothes storage. Rugs and blankets were woven by the women of the family or made from the skin of an animal. A spinning wheel and later a loom might also be found in the main room of the house. This spartan setting was maintained for years - even into the twentieth century.

A large peasant family with six or more children, grandparents, spinster aunts or uncles, and spouses of children could easily have resulted in a dozen or more people living together in a single room. Privacy was obviously completely impossible and therefore all the more sought after - many chose to sleep outside when the weather permitted in order to find space away from the group. It was deathly cold and dark inside in the winter with only the open hearth and a few candles providing heat or light inside a structure that was not waterproof or insulated. Smoke from the fire was a constant inside the house; chimneys were actually nonexistent in the earliest homes. Insects and small vermin were constant companions - often attached to the domestic animals sharing the rooms. While these animals were often welcomed by the family for the additional warmth they could provide in the winter, the smell would have been pungent. All of the senses would have been under constant attack in these early peasant homes.

Kitchens. The kitchen in a Picinisco home was essentially the area surrounding the hearth. Utensils and copper and ceramic pots, kettles, pans and jugs were hung from the roof or walls and terra-cotta storage containers or baskets occupied shelves or the floor. The inside of the hearth had, at its base, several iron stands of various heights to allow for the placement of pots and pans at various distances from the fire for cooking. Sometimes there was an iron bracket at the top of the hearth with hooks for hanging pots for cooking. Often the interior of the hearth had stone ledges built into it allowing for varying temperatures for cooking. Nearby there was a water bucket and dipper, mortar and pestle, and a coffee grinder and pot. Meals were prepared at the kitchen table. Early homes had no baking oven inside the home. Later, ovens were built as a separate stone structure outside and often they were shared with neighbors. Later still, when ovens were built inside the house, they were located within or next to the hearth. In the summer months, because of the heat, the entire cooking operation was moved outside, as were the kitchen table and chairs.

Food and wine was typically stored in a cantina: a cool, dark room, often just a cave or an area excavated from a nearby hill. The cantinas were filled with large wooden barrels full of fermenting grapes, gallons of wine, prosciutto and sausages hanging from the ceiling, cheeses curing, root vegetables, nuts and mushrooms in large baskets, jars of tomato sauce, fruit in large terra-cotta pots and jugs and bottles full of olive oil. Wooden racks hung from the ceiling were loaded with herbs and flowers set to dry.

Homes Within the Town Walls. The earliest townspeople had the distinct advantage of security; their homes were within the thick town walls where they could be defended more easily from man and beast. They also had spiritual comfort from their close proximity to the church. Though these homes shared walls as they lined up next to, or on top of, one another, still they were not weather-resistant. Like their counterparts in the countryside, homes in town

were dark, offered no privacy and were shared with animals brought through large arched doorways. Fuel for the fire had to be transported from nearby woods, though eventually townspeople would utilize the more easily transported coal to heat their homes. Water had to be accessed from town fountains and townspeople shared communal ovens for baking. Their food and marketable crops were grown on plots outside the town walls, requiring them to travel daily to work.

Shepherds' Dwellings on Mountains. In the mountains there were many caves capable of sheltering men and their animals during the summer and shepherds made regular use of these at night and while they were stopped for milking or making cheese. If a natural habitat was not available, shepherds built structures to live in during the summer months and often enclosed them with dry-stone fences for their animals. Harsh winters often caused significant damage to these structures requiring them to be rebuilt year to year. These structures were called "capanne" or "caselle". They included a simple hearth for warmth and cooking and the shepherds slept on the ground with their animals. Some of these structures were circular, almost cone-shaped, like a beehive, such as those used on the plains in Puglia where early shepherds spent the winter months. These were built either entirely of stone or a combination of stone and thatching for the top part of the pyramid. Others were rectangular dry-stone walls with a temporary roof of animal skins or tarp or reeds that needed rebuilding every year.

Chapter 12

Food and Drink

The earliest settlers in Picinisco ate very simply and very little. Meat was scarce, therefore their diet consisted primarily of the vegetables and fruits growing wild in the area, and bread and porridge made from a variety of locally grown cereals or nuts. Food was prepared in a rudimentary fashion due to a lack of kitchen implements and a lack of time to prepare meals. Generally, peasants ate three times a day in winter and four times a day in summer (adding a meal around 4pm in the afternoon). Breakfasts were typically cold and consisted of bread, cheese and fruits. Lunches were cold in the summer when leftovers, salads, fruits, cheeses and bread had to be transported to the workplace. In the evening (and during lunch in the winter) meals were typically a warm soup, with whatever was available put into the pot. Animal fat and olive oil were the typical fats used in meal preparation. Most food had to be preserved as it ripened and stored for consumption throughout the year. Though the people of Picinisco were fortunate to live in a place where they could find food in the wild to supplement their diet, they were keenly aware of the need to ration their food stores to last throughout the year and they were often in danger of malnutrition, particularly in the spring as their winter stores were depleted.

By far the most frequently consumed item in the Comino Valley was polenta – a grain-based porridge. Before the wider production of corn in the 16th century, polenta was made from hulled or crushed grains such as farro, barley, or chickpeas, or from the starchy chestnuts that grew in abundance. Later, corn meal became the staple for polenta. It was a particularly useful dish because leftover polenta could be fashioned into patties and fried, baked or grilled and therefore easily transported. Polenta was eaten at any time of day. Later, when the tomato became available to the Piciniscani, polenta was routinely served with tomato sauce.

Bread was another staple of the diet of the Piciniscani. Each household had to grind flour from chestnuts, barley, wheat, acorns and even potatoes. Taking the grains to one of the mills would have required leaving a portion of the finished flour in payment, so many women ground their own flour. Bread-making was a long and arduous process for the women of Picinisco. After grinding the grain to flour, yeast had to be fermented, dough made and allowed to rise, and then kneaded and formed into loaves. Before the bread could be baked, women had to go to the forests to collect enough wood to fire the ovens and the fires had to be tended for the two or more hours it took to bake the bread. Not a bit of the bread was ever wasted; small pieces were cut off and soaked in milk for teething children, hard crusts were coated with olive oil and garlic for bruschetta, and stale bread was added to thicken vegetable soups. In the eighteenth century, a bread known as "pane casareccio" began to be made with white flour and was crusty on the outside and spongy soft and dense on the inside. People who were away from home, particularly shepherds, might make their bread without yeast in a "coppo" - a terra cotta domed lid with a handle that covered a flat pan allowing the dough to be cooked over an open flame.

Fruit trees were always in abundance in Picinisco and fruit was an important staple of their daily diet. Fruit was also dried or made into preserves to last through the winter months. In addition to fruits and grapes and olives, the Piciniscani cultivated garlic, onions, potatoes, beans and other vegetables in their gardens. The large flocks of sheep and goats meant milk and cheeses were available to supplement the Piciniscani diet too. However, the cultivated fruits and grains and cheeses were also marketable commodities and therefore used only sparingly so they could be sold instead.

Living close to the rich mountainous region meant the Piciniscani could forage for many wild foods: honey, berries, asparagus, spinach, and mushrooms (including truffles) were gathered seasonally by women and children. Salads were made from wild plants like chicory, dandelions, fennel, quinoa, watercress, and rucola. Seasonings like oregano and thyme grew wild and the stems of wild crocuses could be collected and dried for saffron. Nuts of every variety grew wild in the woods: acorns, hazelnuts, chestnuts and walnuts. The people of Picinisco could also fish in local rivers and lakes where the fresh trout was especially known for its flavor, and there were eel and carp as well.

Pasta ultimately also became a staple of the diet of people in the Comino Valley, but likely not on a regular basis until the eighteenth century. Earlier, pasta was used only on special occasions as it required flour and precious eggs and quite a lot of time to prepare, compared to a dish like polenta. Gnocchi, made of potatoes and less time-consuming to prepare, was an early alternative. Pasta was initially used in soups; its use as a separate dish with tomato sauce came later. The tomato was not available in Italy until about the 16th century, and the first recipes to use tomato sauce were written in the seventeenth century. Even then, many thought it was poisonous and physicians warned against its consumption. Not until the late eighteenth and early nineteenth centuries were the tomato cultivated in the Comino Valley, but it quickly became a staple of the peasant diet. Tomato sauce was made at the time of the harvest and meant to last throughout the year. The production of sauce was an all-day affair: the tomatoes had to be boiled, then skinned, and then crushed and salted and placed in jars. Tomato sauce could be used in innumerable ways throughout the year, poured over a plate of polenta, served with pasta, or as a base for a special sauce.

Domestic and wild animals supplemented the diet of the villagers. Chickens provided eggs, lambs were slaughtered and cooked on rare occasions, and a wild pig (or boar) provided prosciutto, pancetta, bacon, and sausage for the family. Up in the mountains there were an abundance of snails in the higher regions that could supply protein. There was also plenty of wild game there, such as hare, quail, gray and red partridge, and grouse and larger animals like deer. However, hunting could only be done with the permission of the feudal landowner, which was presumably not easy to arrange. However, it would have been difficult to catch someone hunting in the vast mountainous region surrounding Picinisco.

Early peasant meals were typically accompanied by wine and even the children would drink a watered-down glass. Picinisco was known for its white wine, although red grapes were also cultivated. In nearby Atina, red grapes are still used to cultivate a DOC wine coveted throughout Italy. Like tomato sauce, the production of wine was meant to last for the entire year. At the harvest, grapes were crushed by foot by the entire family and the mix was poured into a fermenting barrel. When the wine was ready it was stored in the cantina. The Piciniscani liked their wine best when it was unfiltered and fairly young. After-dinner liquors, promoted as an aid to digestion (a "digestivo"), were flavored with the fruits, herbs and nuts gathered nearby.

Holiday Food Traditions. For generations, holiday recipes have been handed down from mother to daughter in Picinisco. Beginning with the first holiday of the calendar year - Carnival - favorite dishes include fried dough recipes like "castagnole", "crustelle", and "cicerchiata". At Easter, the Piciniscani made "pigna" - a panettone-like cake with liqueur and dried fruit, eggs, sugar and lemon zest. They also made "pastone" a dish that looks like a pie (also known as "pizza rustica") made with eggs, ricotta and bacon wrapped in a pastry. In March during the celebration of Saint Joseph's feast day and Father's Day, a dish called "zeppole" is served in Picinisco, often topped with black cherries. Zeppole are little pancakes, round in shape and puffed after cooking (more commonly known as "fritelle" throughout Italy).

The delicacies made to celebrate Christmas included "pizzelle," which is much like the zeppole served in March, but not sweet and typically eaten plain. There is also a pizza that is made with apples, and "calascinetti" a baked dough containing a chestnut puree with chocolate and sugar. For Christmas Eve many cooks make a "tortene," a fried donut covered in sugar. Also "crespelle" (Italian for crepe) is made with a dough mixed with raisins and fried in olive oil; the end result not looking so much like a crepe as a round pastry.

Ice Cream. Ice cream was likely first made in Picinisco during the 1700s. In the middle ages, many people (including physicians) thought that foods of extreme temperatures were bad for one's health. In the Kingdom of Naples, very wealthy individuals looking for the newest culinary creation to serve at their tables began to experiment with frozen concoctions of fruit and cream in the early 1600s. At first the methodology for freezing was a closely guarded secret and remained with the chefs of only the highest nobility. However, by the early 1700s, artists in Naples made the first paintings of Neapolitan street vendors selling ice cream to the masses, so the secret process must have been exposed by then. Snow and ice were already an important commodity in the Kingdom of Naples, subject to regulation and taxation as the demand grew. There are reports that by the early 1800s, Piciniscani shepherds were transporting snow and ice from their mountaintop pastures down to the towns below for sale as a commodity. Certainly traders or visitors would have passed along the recipe for ice cream to people who were in such close proximity to the raw ingredients: fruit, milk, and snow.

Chapter 13

Religion

Catholic Church.   Picinisco's religious life has always been dominated by the Catholic Church.   The first settlement in San Valentino was formed around a monastery and church controlled by the Abbey of Montecassino.   As a landowner, the Church offered settlers a place to establish a home and grow crops, and as a spiritual leader, the Church set values for the community and protected their way of life.   The Catholic Church was thus the first real authority in the area and the townspeople were beholden to the Church for their livelihoods and for the safety and well-being of their families - a symbiotic relationship that ensured complete loyalty to the Church on the part of the settlers.

The Church of Santa Maria Assunta was the first religious center for the town of Picinisco.   Early in 1100 AD, the Church of Santa Maria Assunta is identified in a papal bulletin as part of the diocese of the nearby city of Sora, thereby giving the bishop of Sora ultimate jurisdiction over the faithful of Picinisco, as well as the assets of the Church.   Much the same as feudal peasants owed their lords a portion of their harvest, the Church of Santa Maria Assunta owed obedience and annual payments to the diocese of Sora.   In Church records dated in the 1300s, for example, this contribution consisted of: one-fourth of the Church's burial fees, one-fifth of the regular tithes from the community, a shoulder of pork and 2 loaves of bread at Christmas, and a lamb and 2 loaves of bread at Easter.   For his part, the Bishop of Sora was pleased to have the Church under his dominion.   Santa Maria Assunta included the church, an abbot and, from at least the early 1300s, twelve priests in residence.   The first recorded visit of the Bishop of Sora to Picinisco was in 1305.   The Church of Santa Maria was one of the largest religious communities in the diocese of Sora at that time.   Perhaps it is no surprise then to find that, in the records of the Abbey of Montecassino from this period, four of the Abbey's monks were from Picinisco.

Church of San Lorenzo

The Church of San Lorenzo, now the main center of religious life for the Piciniscani, began life as a small chapel of the Church of Santa Maria Assunta. Its location in the center of the town was much easier to reach than the Church of Santa Maria Assunta, located outside the town walls and down a steep hill. Over time, San Lorenzo was enlarged and began to maintain its own monastery, independent of the Church of Santa Maria Assunta. In the 1500s, the Bishop of Sora formally recognized the Church of San Lorenzo as the main center of religious life for the town and Saint Lorenzo became the patron saint of the Piciniscani. From that point on, the Church of Santa Maria Assunta only held mass on two feast days a year. Many other churches were established in the hamlets surrounding Picinisco, beginning as early as the 1300s. Some were private chapels built by wealthy families, others were financed by contributions from neighbors.

All of these churches offered the "blessings of Catholicism" to those who followed their teachings. Birth was celebrated with baptism, young children made their first confession and first communion, marriage was approved during a religious ceremony and death was mourned at a funeral mass, all under guidelines and with the approval of the Church. The Piciniscani were expected to attend mass and confession, as well as celebrations of all religious holidays. The Church provided aid to the poor and fed the hungry, lent money to its congregation, and prevented others from engaging in usurious activities. For its part, the community was very devout. They were in the habit of asking God and the saints for intervention in the success of their herds, their crops and the health of their families, on a daily basis. Shepherds built shrines in the mountains to ensure they could worship everywhere; farmers asked the priest for a blessing over their crops. The townspeople of Picinisco made contributions to build new churches and to maintain the religious community. They readily donated and left legacies of property to the Church. The Church's holdings were quite extensive, even from as early as the 1600s when a detailed inventory was completed. They owned property outright, shares of harvests or mill outputs, and annual cash contributions. Most all of the priests grew up in Picinisco and their families continued their economic support, even after they joined the priesthood.

Priests were held in high regard in Picinisco. In virtually every historical description of important people in the community, the list of priests dominates the pages. The clergy was supported by brotherhoods of laymen (in 1588, there is a record of what was likely the first brotherhood: the Confratanza di Santa Maria) and, eventually, a group of nuns who established a home and nursery school in Picinisco in the late 1800s. The clergy interacted with the community on a daily basis: administering sacraments, training young people and dealing with church properties. Their constant presence in the daily lives of the Piciniscani enabled the clergy to keep a close watch on the community. Being censured by a priest could result in public shaming in a community like Picinisco that valued religious obedience. In some communities in the Kingdom of Naples the same standard of behavior was not always required of the priests themselves. During the middle ages, it was not uncommon for priests to break their vows of celibacy and father children the community had to support. Priests were forbidden to gamble, dance, carry weapons, dress inappropriately or to practice magic, but often these were offenses were overlooked by the community, unless the infractions were too numerous or particularly egregious. Whether such behavior ever existed in Picinisco is unknown, though perhaps unlikely given the reverence given to the priests of Picinisco through history.

Over the years of Catholic dominance in southern Italy, there were several points of conflict between the Church and the crown in

Naples, as well as with local government and the community at large.   Religious tribunals claimed jurisdiction over all matters relating to the Church, from the misbehavior of clergy to controversies over Church property to sacramental offenses, such as adultery, by people in the community. The secular authorities in Naples believed religious tribunals were too lenient in punishing adultery and asserted this was properly a question for the state, not the Church. Eventually these religious tribunals were abolished by Napoleon. Another controversy involved the amount of land owned by the Catholic Church and how much of it was unproductive. The Church controlled close to one-third of all land in the Kingdom of Naples during the Middle Ages. Productive farmland was not well managed by the Church because it was contributed in "mortmain," meaning it could not be sold and its usage could not be changed. People who left property to the Church to finance prayers for the departed wanted to insure their prayers would continue in perpetuity, so they left the property tied up in mortmain.   This deprived the crown and local governments of significant tax revenue from property that was never developed.

For the congregation at large, there were other points of conflict. The Church was a bureaucracy that needed money and expected its members to make regular contributions of their meager incomes. Yet the clergy wore elaborate robes and were well-fed and the churches were furnished with candlesticks made of silver. Picinisco's church-run hospital for the poor and sick (opened in the late 1500s) owned a long list of income-producing properties, but had only a single room and a single bed to offer to the community. The Church had strict rules about interaction between the sexes and about excessive drinking which parishioners disliked.   The Church occasionally supported (or even colluded with) the feudal lord, to the detriment of the townspeople.   The Church was completely exempt from taxation. One historic record indicates that the bishop of Sora authorized the Church of San Lorenzo to publicly disgrace those townspeople who owed the church money by nailing a list of their names to the door of the church, certainly a less than charitable approach to its congregation.

Perhaps it is not surprising then that the dominance of the Catholic Church declined in the nineteenth and twentieth centuries. The Church was forced to forfeit a great number of its properties. It relinquished its role as educator when public education become available to everyone in the early 1800s. A division of church and state followed Italian unification and the power of the Vatican declined. In the modern era, legalization of divorce and abortion were inevitable. Since the Church no longer held significant power over the advancement of the individual in the community, eventually its role as a spiritual advisor was all that remained. However, the devotion of the Piciniscani remains strong, even today. Huge gatherings of people attend the annual celebration of the patron saint of the town in August each year. The entire community happily gathers together for religious holidays throughout the year. The celebration of sacraments, like first communion, is a community-wide event.

Religious Pilgrimages. Religious pilgrimages were always important to the faithful of southern Italy who believed that a visit to a holy shrine could improve their chances for God's benevolent intervention in their lives. Near Picinisco there is an important religious site that attracts a great many pilgrims from around the world to the area - the Sanctuary of Santa Maria di Canneto (actually located in the comune of neighboring Settefrati). The Sanctuary is thought to have existed as early as the third or fourth century BC, as a place of pagan worship of the Goddess Mefite, a goddess of water and fertility. It first appears in Catholic Church records in 819AD. It is located in the valley of Canneto - high up among the beech trees, in the foothills of Mount Meta where the River Melfa begins above Picinisco. A small chapel/monastery located there was enlarged in the 1400s and has continued to be renovated since that time. From the town of Picinisco, it is at least a three-hour walk to the Sanctuary. The people of Picinisco and many religious pilgrims from around the world, make the climb in August each year for the festival of the Madonna di Canneto. The first written evidence of such a pilgrimage from Picinisco to Canneto is dated in 1639.

The legend of the miracle of Canneto is the story of Silvana, the shepherdess. According to the legend, Silvana was grazing her sheep up on the mountain one day when a lady (the Virgin Mary) appeared to her and told her to go immediately to the priest at Settefrati and tell him he must build a church dedicated to Mary, the mother of Jesus. Silvana was concerned that she needed to find water for her flock before she departed. The lady put her hand on a rock and a spring of water came out allowing Silvana to leave immediately. Silvana then ran to the town to tell everyone about the miracle the lady had performed, causing water to spring out of a rock. The few who followed her back to the site found a statue where the lady had been and knelt down and began to pray there.

Later, other villagers found them in prayer and decided to try to move the statue back to the village, but it was too heavy. When they leaned the statue of the lady against a rock to rest, the head of the statue left an impression in the stone, which stone became known as the "Capo della Madonna". There is also a wooden statue of the Madonna maintained at the Sanctuary, thought to have been carved as early as 1100 or 1200AD, that is called the "Black Madonna" (Madonna Nera) or "Little Dark One" because the face of both the madonna and child have dried to a dark color after years of varnishing.

Vecchia Religione - Magic. In Picinisco the "vecchia religione" functioned side-by-side with the formalities of Catholicism. Prayer was one way to address misfortune, but it was not the only way. Local "faith healers" were known to be successful in healing various maladies. Among those faith healers were people thought to have wider abilities as "witches". The presence of witchcraft (or supernatural powers) was supported by local legends and fables, many of which the Piciniscani clearly understood to be untrue, but which nevertheless lent support to the less extreme instances of magic in the community. These witches possessed the power to protect against the "evil eye," arrange "curses," and assist in matters of the heart with a love potion.

The evil eye or "malocchio" was a method of causing bodily harm or misfortune to another person simply by looking at them with evil intent. Most often the evil eye was cast accidentally, due to some inadvertent expression of envy. People who were thought to be most susceptible to these accidental castings were the weaker elements of society - children and the elderly. To avoid the evil eye, it was considered essential to wear an amulet at all times. Humans, livestock and even a whole house could be protected by an amulet. Some amulets were necklaces: coral in the shape of a horn (the "cornetto"), or an old arrowhead or a specially shaped stone. Others were simply a pouch filled with things said to possess magical qualities. Many superstitions arose from fear of the evil eye. For example, one was not supposed to say a new baby was beautiful because this would cause the child to be cursed with bad luck. A pregnant woman should not wrap wool into a ball of yarn because her child would be born with the umbilical cord wrapped around his neck. One should never refuse a drink from one's own well or the well would dry out.

If something bad happened, the victim could try to avoid the ill-effects of the malocchio by immediately spitting three times in another direction or reciting a blessing. If that did not work, the victim could go to the local "strega" (a witch, also known as a "fattucchiere") to find out what type of evil he or she was faced with. This might be done by putting drops of oil in water and "reading" the drops. An unintentional malocchio could be removed with a simple spell. The more serious, purposefully aggressive, malocchio was more problematic. The witch could either curse the perpetrator (to inflict grave illness or to ruin a harvest) or cast a spell to remove the curse. The witch might try hypnosis, or offer an incantation of incomprehensible words, or create a potion to inflict or combat a curse. Potions were made with the powder of dried worms, spider webs, urine, the skin of a snake, hair of a badger, an olive branch or local metals. Sometimes the potion was put into a small bag and burned while repeating an incantation. Often an incantation would invoke the assistance of one or more saints. The power of the witch was taken very seriously, and even today many of the superstitions surrounding the malocchio and other evil actions are followed by members of the community.

Chapter 14

Relationship Between the Sexes

The earliest influence on the relationship between the sexes in Picinisco was the Catholic Church, and the Church taught that the act of sex was permitted only for those who were married and only for purposes of procreation. The Church's goal was to preserve the virginity of the town maidens so they could be properly married. In addition to protecting their persons, the Church protected women against potential poverty by prohibiting divorce and offering protection from sexual harassment through the Church's convents. To lessen the temptation of sex out of wedlock, the Church supported very limited freedom for women; unmarried men and women could not meet together except in the presence of the community or the priest. Although men had greater freedom of movement in the community, the threat of being cut off by the Church was a forceful deterrent to unacceptable behavior.

From the beginning, marriages in Picinisco were typically arranged by parents and most of them were not anxious to have their children (who were sometimes their principal source of labor) leave home (even into the twentieth century). Choices were limited by social and economic status since marriages outside this parameter would not be approved by the Church, the feudal lord or the community. Even by the early 1800s, the profession of the bride and groom's parents was quite often exactly the same. Usually, choices were made among families who had known one another for generations and were worked out when children were young. Parental selections may have considered attachments between young boys and girls, but were just as likely to be made for economic advantage to the parents and this practice remained in effect even through the early 1900s. As it gradually became more acceptable for young people to form their own romantic attachments, they still needed the approval of their parents.

Once an arrangement had been made there was still time for the young woman to express her own preferences (if her family allowed it). The groom and one or two friends would go to the bride's home late at night and sing love songs beneath her window accompanied by a guitar, mandolin or organ. These songs were designed to show the bride the extent of the groom's feelings for her and the bride could light a candle in her window to indicate her acceptance. If the potential groom was not acceptable, he might be doused with a bucket of water from the young woman's window and the entire neighborhood would witness the young man's rejection. Breaking an arranged engagement was thought to be extremely offensive. The potential bride and groom and all of their relatives broke off all contact with one another. For the young woman, it was particularly devastating. It was almost impossible to find another spouse for her and she remained in her father's home as a spinster, humiliated.

If the groom was acceptable, his parents would make a formal application to the parents of the potential bride and they would all enter into negotiations about her dowry. Since the bride was to become completely dependent on her husband, it was thought to be only proper for her to bring certain things to her marriage. The dowry might include jewelry, household linens embroidered by the bride, mattresses, copper cooking utensils, terra cotta pots, tools for the hearth, glasses, cutlery, equipment for bread-making, etc. Sometimes there was land to be bartered over as well. A "difficult" bride (headstrong in personality, or not necessarily beautiful in appearance) might require extra in the way of a dowry to make the match acceptable. A few days before the wedding a group of women would follow the groom through the streets of Picinisco to the couple's new home carrying all of the bride's dowry in big baskets. In part this was to assure the community the full dowry had been given, but in part it may have been to inspire some envy. For girls who could not afford a dowry or even a dress to be married in, there was a special fund, created by a wealthy landowner in 1707, called the Monte Maritaggi, that might be of assistance. Once a year in June, the priest gathered the names of the eligible girls, ages 13 to 25, who were poor and honest and who had no sisters who had benefited from the Monte Maritaggi for 13 years. The girl selected had to be married within the year to take advantage of the monetary prize. The prize is still awarded today.

The priest posted the marriage banns in the church and stated the intentions at mass. Generally, Saturday was considered the best day of the week for a wedding; a Tuesday or Friday was considered bad luck. Also, weddings were generally not arranged for November (when the community celebrated the dead), nor during Lent. In the early 1800s, most marriages were between people in their mid-twenties or older. On the day of her wedding the bride was dressed in white, or in a special dress purchased by the groom for the occasion, and presented to her future mother-in-law for her public approval. The groom arrived at the church first, accompanied by his mother and the rest of his family. The bride paraded through the streets of town with her family and entered the church on the arm of her father. Years ago, as the bride and groom came together for the ceremony, they held a handkerchief between them instead of holding hands. After the ceremony, the guests would throw coins and confetti and the couple would parade through the streets to the home of, usually, the groom for the celebration. There they would be fed and there would be dancing and singing and music. After the feast the couple would go to their wedding bed, which had been decorated with confetti and sugared almonds, and wedding guests would enter the room and leave gifts for the couple, typically coins, on their marital bed.

Apart from the dictates of the Catholic Church, the legal status of women in the Kingdom of Naples ensured their almost complete subservience to men. Women could not make a will, could not bring a lawsuit, could not make accusations at a criminal trial, and could not enter into a contract. Men could legally override any decision a wife made about marriages for children, dealing with dowry property, or even opening a bank account. Women had to give men all of their wages. If a woman's husband neglected her or failed to provide food or shelter for her and her children, her only option was to complain to the priest. She could not compel his support in court nor legally divorce him. Likewise, if a woman's husband beat her or molested her, she had no absolutely recourse under the law.

A woman molested by someone other than her husband was not considered to be a "victim" in the Kingdom of Naples. Rather, her family's honor was the victim of a crime and the male members of her family were empowered to seek retribution. If the woman was unmarried, one possible solution was to extract a payment equivalent to a dowry from the perpetrator. Another solution was to require the perpetrator to marry the victim. The woman had no right to approve or disapprove these solutions. Should the male members of a woman's family commit murder in defense of the family's honor, the "delitto d'onore" defense (honor killing) decreed that the murderer was excused from punishment. Adultery was generally considered a crime committed by women, dishonoring their husbands. In the twelfth and thirteenth centuries, adultery was punished by slitting the woman's nose, unless her husband objected to this disfigurement, in which case she would flogged instead. There were even instances where a husband was charged as a criminal if he discovered his wife was an adulterer and failed to punish her. In Picinisco, the accepted treatment of an adulterous woman was to yank her out of her house by her hair and throw her into the streets of town where she would be publicly shamed. Because an accusation of infidelity could be made solely by a husband, women could be falsely accused by a husband who was jealous or a bully.

In the 1800s, as women began to receive more education and joined the workforce in greater numbers, they began to push for legal protection of women's rights. Widows and abandoned wives became eligible to deal with family property and their children, though married women had to wait until the 1970s for equality of power within the marriage. Women were allowed to be witnesses in court and to write a will. A proposal for women to have the vote was first made in 1867, though women had to wait until 1947 when it was finally allowed. Adultery continued as a crime committed by women, but after Italian unification a man could be charged with adultery. However, the man was only guilty if he kept another woman in his marital home or flagrantly maintained her in another dwelling. Adultery was finally decriminalized in the 1960s. The defense of "honor killing" was enacted into law in the early 1800s, with the expansion of the list of those who could be killed and the addition of a reduced sentence for the perpetrator. Essentially, the law provided that the murder of any person who molested a wife, daughter or sister, or the murder of the molested wife, daughter or sister, motivated by family honor, could result in punishment of no more than 3 to 5 years. The "honor killing excuse" was later incorporated into the criminal code in post-unification Italy, where it remained on the books until 1981. Finally, in the 1970s, Italy legalized divorce and abortion

It is not surprising then that the relationship between men and women was for hundreds of years one of basically master and servant. Women were taught, from a very young age, that they were subservient to men. At home, women used the polite "voi" form of Italian to address their fathers, husbands and even brothers. Kissing the hand of the elder man of the house was required. Women and girls served meals to the men of the house first and often only men were permitted to eat at the table. Females were not allowed to travel alone and their socialization was limited to the company of other women. A pregnancy out-of-wedlock resulted in the complete ruin of the woman. Many times unwanted children were simply abandoned to avoid public shaming. Several births and deaths registered in the early 1800s in Picinisco have no mother or father listed. The child is given the last name of "Proietta" or "Projetti", signifying the baby's abandonment. This apparently comes from the Latin word "proicere" meaning "to be abandoned." The birth was typically reported by a midwife or priest. The abandonment of babies was a regular occurrence into the nineteenth century, whether resulting from illegitimacy or from poverty.

Over time this complete subservience has changed. Men and women are free to marry whomever they choose. Legally, women have rights equal to those of men. Women work and have independent economic lives and control over their bodies. Women serve in the national and local legislatures: in Picinisco a woman sits on the town council. Still, Italy remains a conservative, patriarchal society and women continue to work for equality on all fronts.

Chapter 15

Medical Attention

A thousand years ago people generally believed that a medical problem, whether it was a broken leg or a mysterious disease, occurred because God was displeased with them in some way or was presenting them with a trial to test their devotion. Thus, to avoid medical problems one needed to be devout. If a medical problem did arise, the first thing a person did was to go the priest and ask for his help and prayers. This was true whether the patient was human or animal - both were treated in exactly the same manner. But the Piciniscani were not content to leave the matter solely to spiritual intervention (in the same way that their commitment to Catholicism did not prevent them from embracing the superstitions of the "vecchia religione"). If a family was unable to find its own remedy, they could and did consult local healers known to have dealt successfully with particular medical problems. Some of these healers were charlatans using only spells and incantations to heal. However, even at this early date, certain people living in Picinisco were known to have successfully treated specific ailments and the community did not hesitate to use them.

During the medieval period, there were significant advances in medical science, many with the support of the Catholic Church. The great abbeys began establishing libraries and collecting treatises from around the world in furtherance of knowledge on a variety of topics, including medicine. This new focus on "scientific study" was ultimately embraced by the entire educational community. Serious medical training was then implemented in the curriculum of university learning. It was also possible to practice medicine after a term as an apprentice to another doctor, who then certified the "doctor's" credentials after some basic training. Still, it took time and money to train as a physician - two things in short supply in Picinisco.

By the late 1500s, there were several types of medical attention available to the population. The various medical service providers were outlined in a law enacted by the Kingdom of Naples to tax medical services: physicians, surgeons, barbers, bone-setters, apothecaries, herbalists and mid-wives. In 1595, Picinisco had at least one medical doctor and a surgeon living in the town. Medical doctors or physicians dealt primarily with illness and disease, while surgeons dealt primarily with accidental injuries. The "surgeon" of this time was often a "barber-surgeon." Barbers, who shaved, cut hair, trimmed beards and offered manicures, possessed the tools - clean, sharp knives and razors - of surgery and an expertise in their use that allowed them to develop a skill in surgical-like procedures. They performed amputations, lanced abscesses and often dealt with dental issues. They also practiced the procedure of "blood-letting", a process of opening a vein and extracting blood from a sick person to drain noxious forces or poison from the system. Even into the nineteenth century, this was an acceptable medical treatment for a person with a heart attack. Often leeches were used in blood-letting and applied to the part of the body that was thought to be injured until they were full of blood and fell off the body, when the poison was presumed to be removed.

Of course there was a cost to seeing a medical doctor or a barber-surgeon, who might prescribe medicine or a procedure as a treatment, adding to the expense. Many people in Picinisco would not have been able to afford such a luxury. Herbalists, most often women familiar with the medicinal uses of plants, offered a more affordable alternative. The mountainous region of Picinisco contained many plant remedies that actually had medicinal properties. In fact, the apothecaries of large metropolitan areas like Naples were importing medicinal plants from Picinisco for their own use in the middle ages. Probably the most common wild plant in use in Picinisco for medicinal purposes was "mallow." Local herbalists prescribed mallow for its anti-inflammatory properties, particularly in treating gastrointestinal problems. Mallow was also regularly prescribed for dermatitis, toothache and dental abscesses, coughs, bronchitis, and sore throats and, in its dried form, it was used for colic, abdominal pain, and as a laxative.

Another common plant-medicine was chamomile, whose flowers were steeped to create a tea or whose essential oils were extracted and given orally. Chamomile was prescribed as a relaxant or sedative (for spasm relief, to induce sleep, ease frayed nerves, anxiety, relax muscles and joints, ease menstrual cramps and backaches or an upset stomach) or for its anti-inflammatory properties. Herbalists recommended bitter root, another locally available herb, to prepare a tonic to fight malaria, to deal with digestive track issues, arthritis, and jaundice. They also recommended bitter root be applied to a wound to facilitate healing. Nettles, which were very popular in food preparation, were prescribed as a remedy for hair loss and their leafy branches were recommended for use as a scrub brush for aching arms and legs or joints inflamed with rheumatism to relieve suffering.

Childbirth was, of course, the province of a midwife and her knowledge was typically passed down from generation to generation. A Piciniscani midwife would combine her quasi-medical approach (gleaned from her attendance at hundreds of births) with attention to widely-held superstitions about the birthing process. For example, the Piciniscani believed that for a good birth, only women should be in the room with the pregnant woman and that no one who had a deformity should be present. Piciniscani women believed that the pain of childbirth could be taken away by wiping the expectant mother with a red cloth. Midwives were consulted for a variety of women's health issues. A knowledgeable midwife might prescribe juniper to prevent abortion and other fern varieties to promote menstruation. Away from the prying eyes of the priest, part of the yew tree or a form of wild cucumber could be prescribed by the midwife to cause a miscarriage. A good midwife would be consulted by everyone in the community, regardless of social class divisions between them.

Remedies for day to day health issues were well-known by the community. Garlic was used to prevent worms in humans and animals, onions were used as a poultice for coughs and colds, potatoes were cut open and placed on burns, and lemons were used to treat headaches or sinus issues. Wine was a common treatment, particularly for coughs and colds, boiled and reduced to a thick liquid toddy for patients. Mint was used as an insect repellant for humans and animals alike.

The Kingdom of Naples regulated medical care in a piecemeal fashion (reacting to events like the plague of 1656 only after literally hundreds of thousands of people had died). Attention to public health issues affecting the Kingdom was virtually non-existent in Naples, leaving local authorities or the Catholic Church to deal with widespread medical problems. The Università in Picinisco paid for the services of a medical doctor, but it is unclear who was entitled to use the doctor's services and just what type of ailments the doctor was qualified to treat. In the early 1800s, there were several qualified medical providers practicing in Picinisco and the prosperity of the community likely meant medical treatment was more readily available. After Italian unification in the late 1800s, a system of national health care was adopted for all of Italy. Even then, however, the closest hospitals to Picinisco were in Sora and Cassino, both more than 30 kilometers away. The state of transportation, even into the twentieth century, was such that the trip might take a day or more to accomplish. Thankfully today there is a doctor and pharmacy in town and the nearest hospitals are a short drive away.

Chapter 16

Education

When Picinisco was founded in the eleventh century, very few people in Italy were formally educated. The peasantry had no time for nor access to education. The local clergy memorized the Latin needed to recite the mass, but did not really need to understand the language to minister to their peasant congregation. The nobility, who had the money and time for education, did receive some instruction, but at this early stage in history, education was based on a study of the classics and did not address practical subjects like science and math. Even so, we know that in the eleventh century there were people in Picinisco who had some training. A judge and notary were involved with the land transfer of 1054AD. Judges of this time period were empowered to resolve matters such as local contracts and inheritance questions, a position obviously requiring some ability to read and write. Likewise, the notary, who was entrusted with writing down contracts, typically in Latin, would have been an educated person. Both the notary and the judge served at the pleasure of feudal lords who were sufficiently wealthy to have been educated, at least to some extent. But the peasants who witnessed the land transfer and signed their names with an "X" represented the overwhelming majority of the uneducated populace of this time.

Religious training was the first form of education in Picinisco. In 1347 there were colleges for the training of new priests established by the Church of Santa Maria Assunta, at its chapels of San Lorenzo and San Nicolo. This is one of the earliest records of educational training available in all of the Comino Valley. Although such education was likely fairly rudimentary, it is possible some of the educators were themselves trained at the nearby Abbey of Montecassino, known as a center of learning with a keen interest in education. St. Thomas Aquinas, born in 1225 to a noble family in the nearby town of Roccasecca, was sent to the Montecassino Abbey at the age of 5 to begin his education. In general, however, the training of priests was not particularly rigorous in these early years. It was not until the 1600s that seminaries were founded to institute a higher standard of education. Seminaries in nearby Sora or Caserta, or even Naples, eventually attracted scholars from the Comino Valley seeking a broader education.   Young Picinisco native Ernesto Capocci (who became a world-renowned astronomer) began his formal education early in the 1800s at the seminary in Sora.   Some Jesuit schools were established in the Kingdom of Naples in the late 1500s to educate the poor, but none were located near Picinisco.   Religious educational opportunities continued to be important to the people of Picinisco through the nineteenth century, as many of its professionals (doctors, lawyers, authors) received their initial training from the Catholic community.

Non-religious education was not universally available in the Kingdom of Naples until the nineteenth century.   In Alvito, the capital city of the Duchy of which Picinisco was a part, there is evidence that the università there had an official spot for a teacher as early as the middle 1500s.   However, there were no particular qualifications for the "maestro" and frequently no money to pay for such a position.   In 1632, two such teachers are listed in the records of Alvito, though none are reported in any of the other towns of the Duchy.   In the mid-1700s, the King of Naples attempted to establish a new system of public education for the Kingdom that would exclude any religious influence.   However, his decree required new schools be financed by local town governments and smaller towns like Picinisco did not have the money or the commitment of its population to fund a school.

In the early 1800s, the Napoleonic reforms included legislation abolishing the piecemeal system of church and state education and mandated a secular education for all citizens of the Kingdom. Following this legislation, a primary school was introduced in Picinisco in 1808.   The municipality decided to hire a male and female schoolteacher whose wages would be paid from taxes imposed on the townspeople.   In 1811, Lorenzo Boni was the schoolmaster for boys and Caterina Bartolomucci was hired to teach the girls.   However, it took years for the parents of school-aged children to be convinced that the benefits of education outweighed the loss of manpower to the family.   In 1819, there is a report that not a single girl had enrolled in the school in Picinisco since Ms. Bartolomucci was hired.   The local priests were implored to preach the benefits of education to the community and in particular to advise fathers of the importance of education for their daughters.

Higher education was available at the University of Naples (established in the 1200s, but not fully functioning until the 1500s) for someone with the wealth or patronage of a benefactor to support their education, provided they also had the time to devote to education. Clearly a handful of people in Picinisco were able to access some education; written reports from the early 1600s indicate that there were notaries, two doctors of law, a doctor of medicine and a surgeon living in town, as well as other professionals who practiced outside of Picinisco after their training. Still, they represented just a fraction of the total population. By the early 1800s, more people were routinely training at the University of Naples and many returned to Picinisco to practice their professions.

In the first census taken after Italian unification the national government surveyed the level of illiteracy in Italy. In the province of Terra di Lavoro, where Picinisco is located, the illiteracy rate was 88%. In an 1862 report on the schools operating in Picinisco, for example, there were 172 pupils, slightly more boys than girls, in 4 schools - two for boys and two for girls - with a staff of four teachers. The total population of the town at that time was in excess of 3,200 people; it seems likely that many more than 5% of the population were school-aged children, so participation was obviously still very limited.

Not surprisingly, following unification a new law was passed mandating primary school attendance for all boys and girls in every community. It took some time for the state to begin implementing the law. By 1869, the first three levels of elementary schooling had been implemented throughout Italy. It was not until 1923 that a fourth grade level was added and in 1937 a fifth level was added. Then, in the 1950s, levels six through eight were added, generally requiring students up to age 14 to attend school. Today, education is compulsory for ages 6 to 16. Picinisco has an elementary school located in the town and students aged 11 and older travel to nearby towns for secondary school.

Chapter 17

Calamitous Events in Picinisco

Natural Disasters. The central Italian Apennine chain of mountains where Picinisco is located is and always has been one of the most active seismic areas in Europe. Even today, earthquakes occur quite regularly. The earliest recorded earthquake to have done significant damage to the town of Picinisco was on September 9, 1349. This very large earthquake caused serious damage in many of the towns of the Comino Valley, and as far away as the Abbey at Montecassino. Neighboring Atina was almost completely destroyed by this earthquake. In fact, the Aquino family feudal lord who reigned over much of the Comino Valley during this period died in that earthquake.

Significant earthquakes were also recorded in the Comino Valley in 1456 and again in 1654. In the earthquakes of 1805 and 1809, the castle in Picinisco suffered damage and had to be partially rebuilt. The next very large earthquake occurred in 1873: two homes in Picinisco were completely destroyed and 52 others had to be evacuated due to the large cracks affecting their foundations. Other minor earthquakes were recorded in Picinisco in 1876 and 1891.

The earthquake of January 15, 1915 was one of the largest ever recorded in the area, killing over 30,000 people. The worst damage in the Comino Valley occurred slightly to the east of Picinisco; nevertheless, there was serious damage to the historic town center. Seventy years later, the epicenter of the May, 1984 earthquake was San Donato Valcomino, literally right next door to Picinisco. Picinisco's historical center was significantly damaged in this earthquake as well. The Church of San Lorenzo suffered significant damage, as did the Church of San Rocco in the piazza.

There are other unusual weather events that have occurred in the region. In 1761, a large hurricane hit the coast of Naples and a tremendous amount of rain accompanying that hurricane fell as far away as the Comino Valley. In Picinisco, there were huge landslides that caused damage to the town and surrounding areas, particularly to the roads in the area. Many people lost their lives as well. One effect of this landslide was the creation of a small lake which, over the next 20 years, supplied trout and eel to the community. Then, in the 1880s, another large landslide occurred causing the lake to completely disappear.

There are innumerable incidents of drought and other natural disasters that caused famine in the Comino Valley, beginning with the earliest recorded histories. During the famine of 1763/64, following a huge drought, food became so scarce that animals could not be fed and livestock was lost. The government in Naples had to step in to regulate grain prices. Any famine in the countryside would have even more disastrous effects for the city-dwellers who relied on produce from outlying farms. In the middle of this famine, Tolomeo Gallio, then the Duke of Alvito, ignored the starving people in the Duchy and decided to impose an even larger tax burden on them to improve his own suffering coffers.

Disease. It is assumed that a ship docking in Naples brought the bubonic plague to southern Italy in 1656. Although travel was eventually curtailed, it was done too late and the plague spread across the Kingdom like wildfire. Close to half of the population of the city of Naples was lost to the plague. Though the Comino Valley was isolated in terms of geography, every town suffered losses. Population figures for Picinisco before and after the plague show a 35% reduction. The next-door town of Settefrati was completely abandoned after the devastating effects of the plague and people did not return there for years afterwards. Many blame the gatherings at weekly mass for the spread of the plague in the Comino Valley.

In 1874, an epidemic of cholera reached the Comino Valley town of San Biagio di Saracinisco, located some eight miles from Picinisco. 300 people died in San Biagio that year from cholera. Though there are no specific written references to the presence of cholera in Picinisco (it is possible they closed the town off to prevent its spread), the population did decline by 10% between 1870 and 1880. This may be explained by the beginning of significant waves of emigration from Picinisco, but cholera would have been, at the very least, a huge worry for the population of Picinisco.

Man-Made Disasters. Fire was always a risk in a small town but since Picinisco was constructed largely of stone, the risk was slightly diminished. Nevertheless, in 1600 there was a fire that caused all of the parochial records of the Church of San Lorenzo to be destroyed. (Having spent time hunting through these records I am not surprised to hear there was a fire. The first volume of the remaining church records was partially ruined by what looks like the remains of a candle left burning on the book!).

The Piciniscani suffered in times of war as well. During the feudal period, men could be called to military service by their feudal lord who was bound to support the king in armed conflicts as part of his feudal obligations. In the early 1800s, national service was imposed in the Kingdom of Naples and the peasantry fought bitterly against this policy. All men between the ages of 18 and 25 were obliged to serve. However, wealthy individuals could buy an exemption by arranging a substitute to serve in their place. Following the unification of Italy, military service was required on behalf of the newly united country. In addition to military service, many lost their lives at the hands of brigands based in the nearby mountains. Beginning in the middle ages right through Italian unification in 1860 and for 10 years after, many were called to fight or attacked by these gangs.

Both world wars in the twentieth century spelled disaster for many Piciniscani. During World War I, the government required military service from the younger men in the community, but by the end of the war even the elderly were called into service. Over 500 of the 3000 residents of Picinisco served in the war, leaving many women and children to fend for themselves for many years. Of those who did serve, 47 died and 14 were crippled. In World War II, 11 men died and 18 were crippled while serving in the military. There were also 56 civilians killed or maimed in Picinisco during World War II. Italians, including many Piciniscani, living in Great Britain during World War II suffered as well. They were branded as "enemy aliens" of Britain, despite the fact that they had been living there for years and even had sons serving in the British army. Britain determined to intern enemy aliens in Canada and in June of 1940, over 700 interned Italian men boarded a ship called the Arandora Star sailing for Canada. The ship was sunk by German U-boats and, of the 1564 people on board, approximately 730 died, including 446 Italians. Possibly as many as 80 of the Italians killed on the Arandora Star were from the Comino Valley; 18 of them were from Picinisco.

Like the brigandage of earlier years, World War II happened right on the doorstep of the town of Picinisco. Mussolini was ousted from control in Italy in July, 1943 and the Italian government surrendered to the Allies in August, leaving the Germans to defend the country. The Allies landed in southern Italy in September, 1943 to begin advancing north to Rome. As the Allies advanced from the south, the Germans put a series of fortified lines together in southern Italy, including the Gustav Line following the Liri Valley near Picinisco. A detachment of German soldiers was sent to occupy Picinisco in October, 1943 and the townspeople were ordered to provide them with everything they needed. Initially, the Germans were friendly towards the local population. When the German high command ordered raiding parties to look for men of serviceable age who were in hiding or for animals to feed the troops, the resident Germans gave the Piciniscani advance notice of the hunt. But friendly relations did not last long. Food soon became scarce and the Germans raided the gardens and orchards of Picinisco, laughing off any request for payment (15,000 sheep were confiscated in the Comino Valley alone). As the Piciniscani realized the Germans would take literally everything they had, they began to hide all of their possessions, digging holes in the ground to bury them or walling off a small corner of the house to hide them. The Germans also ordered the Piciniscani to produce various Jewish citizens suspected of hiding in Picinisco. Fortunately, the Jewish families had gone into hiding in the mountains before they could be arrested, but the Germans still required the townspeople to form search parties and spend time in the mountains looking for them.

The Allies hoped to break through the Gustav Line and proceed to Rome along a highway that ran by the town of Cassino. But the Germans dug in and the Allies were stalled for months as they tried to break through their defenses. This confrontation ultimately became known as the "Battle of Montecassino." As it began at the end of 1943, one thousand refugees from Cassino and its surrounds were evacuated to Picinisco where there was not enough food to feed them or places to shelter them. German soldiers at the front near Cassino were constantly arriving in Picinisco for a few days of rest and expected food and shelter to be provided by the townspeople. Town buildings were requisitioned for use by the Germans and soldiers roamed the town taking whatever they wanted from the locals. Once the Allies discovered that Picinisco was a resting point for German soldiers, they began bombing the town itself. Shelling started on January 12, 1944. On January 14, 1944, there was a direct hit on the town and a great deal of destruction. When the bombing started anew on January 15th, the German command ordered all the Piciniscani to be evacuated.

The evacuation was immediate and the townspeople who did not escape into the mountains to live in caves or old shepherd huts were taken by trucks to other towns in the area. They arrived without any provisions and nowhere to stay in the dead of winter. The evacuation remained in effect until the Battle of Montecassino ended in May, 1944. When the Piciniscani were allowed to return home, they discovered their homes had been ransacked and their belongings and food were gone. Things they had hidden underground had been dug up and looted by the Germans. As a final insult, the Germans blew up their ammunition dump in the town and mined the road to Atina as they left Picinisco.

Chapter 18

Brigandage

Gangs of brigands roamed the Comino Valley for hundreds of years, primarily because its isolated location and surrounding wild landscape offered them the perfect place to hide and evade capture. "Brigands" were groups of men and sometimes women who lived on the run by violently and mercilessly harassing and robbing travelers and local populations alike. They chose a life of brigandage for different reasons: some were actual thieves and murderers, predisposed to violence, but others joined in reaction to dire economic circumstances or for political reasons. Some brigands operated as quasi-military units and others acted like Robin Hood, purporting to deliver justice to the poor by taking from wealthy landowners and visitors. People in Picinisco were often torn between supporting and even joining the brigands, and fighting to suppress them.

Many people in Picinisco suffered brutally at the hands of these brigands. In the summer, the brigands would surround lonely shepherds on the mountains and hold them and their flocks for ransom. In the winter, they would surround a house, make everyone go outside and tear the house apart taking whatever they wanted. Since these poor people had no cash, the brigands stole their stores of food, clothing, tobacco, blankets, - whatever they had. The gangs left their victims devastated; women and young girls were raped, those who resisted were dealt with violently, and many starved after being robbed of all their food stores.

Though brigandage was always a problem in the Kingdom of Naples, there were four main periods of brigandage that affected the people of Picinisco. The first was at the end of the 1500s when the Spanish ruled the Kingdom of Naples with "viceroys" from Spain who were universally hated as cruel and ruthless leaders. Marco Sciarra, known as the "Re della Campagna" (King of the Countryside) and his group were determined to wreak havoc on these Spanish viceroys. Sciarra and his band of over 600 men and women found a haven in the Apennine mountains near Picinisco where they could easily hide from the Spanish authorities. They claimed to offer the peasants of poor towns their protection from Spanish authorities who were attempting to collect heavy taxes. As a result, they were admired and respected by many locals. At the same time, Sciarra and his group demanded loyalty from the locals and enforced that loyalty with cruel and vicious justice for any who betrayed them. Sciarra became notorious throughout Italy and was hunted by the Spanish government in Naples and the Catholic Church in Rome. He was finally killed in 1593, just as Cardinal Gallio took control of the Duchy and initiated his own determined effort to rid the area of brigandage.

The next wave of brigandage began at the end of the 1700s with the clash between the new French Napoleonic government in Naples and the exiled Spanish government. The "Sanfedista" were local militias who supported the return of the Spanish government to Naples. But instead of being a purely political force, these gangs claimed the right to attack anyone associated with the French. Gaetano Mammone, from nearby Sora, led a particularly bloodthirsty group determined to find and penalize French loyalists on behalf of the exiled Spanish King Ferdinand. Mammone was hailed by the deposed king and by nobles who relied on him for security for their feudal estates.   To the peasants of Picinisco, however, Mammone was a terrorist.   He was accused of cannibalism and of personally killing some 500 people. He was finally killed in 1802.   Another Sanfedista, Michele Pezzo, who became known as "Fra Diavolo," also terrorized the area that included Picinisco.   Even the members of the exiled Spanish government, who supported his efforts, began to think Diavolo was too aggressive. It took the Napoleonic government until 1806 to capture and kill him. Benedetto Panetta, from nearby Villa Latina, served with Fra Diavolo and took up the fight after his death by attacking the nearby town of Atina with 700 men. The attack failed and Panetta was killed a few years later.

After the abolishment of feudal ownership by the Napoleon government in the early 1800s, the next wave of brigandage involved the "Carbonari." The Carbonari were a secret group of zealous, liberal patriots pushing for reform and for Italy's freedom from foreign influence in the years leading up to unification. It seems the villagers of Picinisco generally supported freedom from foreign domination in Naples, but the Carbonari were not always discriminating in their choice of victims and the Piciniscani had to defend their village against random attacks by the Carbonari. Things were so bad by the 1820s that the mayor of Picinisco ordered all of the gates of the city, except the gate to the piazza, to be permanently closed. He posted guards at the piazza gate each night and this defensive posture lasted for many years.

The final wave of brigandage happened once Italy formed a single unified state in 1861. The new national government of Victor Emmanuel seemed to abandon the rural southern peasants who had supported the unification process in exchange for promises of reforms that never happened. Many southern Italian peasants believed they would be better off with the former royal government in Naples than with the unknown Victor Emmanuel. A gang of brigands under the leadership of Luigi Alonzi, called "Chiavone" operated in and around Picinisco until 1863, and was followed by the gang of Domenico Fuoco. Like their predecessors, these men would steal, murder, blackmail, extort, mutilate and otherwise torture the peasants of the area to enforce their loyalty to the brigands over the new national government. The peasants were in a horrible vise - if they supported the government, they suffered at the hands of the brigands, and if they supported the brigands, they were fighting against the new national government.

It took the new government over 10 years to eradicate the brigandage in the south of Italy. Initially they empowered a National Guard to deal with the brigands, a company of which was located in Picinisco under the direction of the battalion leader in nearby Atina. This company had over 100 men and they went each week to Atina to train with other regional companies. This National Guard fought the brigands for almost 5 years before the army was called in to deal with the problem. It took until 1870 for the brigands to be eradicated.

Not surprisingly, the Piciniscani who were members of the National Guard became primary targets for the Chiavone and Fuoco gangs. In one incident, in the winter of 1864, a group of them were out hunting in the mountains near a cave where some brigands were making camp. Spotted by the brigands, the hunters prepared to return fire but both sides were unable to see moments later as a dense fog covered the area. One of the hunters, a bugler for the National Guard, used his horn to pretend to summon imaginary National Guard troops and the brigands quickly disbursed.

Unfortunately, the locals were not always so lucky. In 1865, Alfonso DeMarco, a lieutenant in the National Guard, was hunting in the mountains above Picinisco when he was captured by Fuoco's gang.

The gang demanded a ransom from DeMarco's family under penalty of his death. The family paid the full ransom, again and again, over the next three days. Then, while Fuoco's gang was having their evening meal (of food taken from the DeMarco family), one of the gang members was convinced to loosen DeMarco's ties and DeMarco was able to throw himself off a cliff into deep snow. While being shot at by the gang, DeMarco made his way down the mountain and safely back to town. Meanwhile, Antonio Santangeli, a friend who brought part of the ransom to the Fuoco gang for the DeMarcos, was caught by Fuoco's mistress and brutally stabbed in the stomach by her, dying later the same day. Another Santangeli was captured by Fuoco and kept by the gang for several days before they smashed his head with boulders.

Fuoco was finally killed in 1870 by local men he had captured and was holding for ransom. His gang had rounded up five men; the two richest of them were kept by the gang while the others were released to secure the ransom money. The gang cut off the ears of their prisoners while waiting for the ransom money. When their guards fell asleep one night, the prisoners rose up and the youngest was able to kill Fuoco with an axe to his head. Two other gang members were also killed. The prisoners returned to Picinisco and the National Guard was dispatched to collect the bodies. The bodies were placed on display in Montano Park for two days for all to see. It was a gruesome but welcome sight for the Piciniscani.

Chapter 19

Music and Dancing

Music and dancing have always been an important part of the culture of Picinisco and every aspect of life had its attendant song or dance. The earliest music of Picinisco had a tempo much like a Gregorian chant, as it was based upon music the community heard in church, during mass. But more important than the melody, it was the lyrics of the songs of the Comino Valley that set them apart: these songs dealt with the feelings and circumstances of the everyday life of the Piciniscani. Their lyrics described their environment, both the beauty and the treacherousness of their surroundings; love, both lost and found, fulfilled and unrequited; the harvest, a desire for abundance or request for tolerance from the master if the harvest was wanting; and devotion to God, requests for forgiveness and thanks. Other songs related to the seasons of a farming existence: planting, harvesting, winters of scarcity. There are also lyrics dealing with the lives of shepherds far from home, concerned about predators and the success of the transumanza and about their families left alone during their travels. Still other songs celebrate particular holidays, such as Easter and Christmas, or feast days of local saints.

Many of the songs of the Piciniscani use the same melody. Often they are sung by a group, as a round or in parts. A shepherd up on the mountain might begin a tune about his flock and be answered by another nearby shepherd, who might add his own verse. In the fields, as the farmer and his family worked the rows of grain, they might call out to one another in song about their hope for the harvest and be answered by singers in the next row. Singing certainly helped to pass the time but it was also a means of telling stories and passing along information. Women who gathered to bake bread or do their washing might sing songs that would inform the community that a young girl was ready for marriage, or relate the story of an unfortunate woman who let a good man slip away from her. Many of the songs popular in Picinisco had no title but the ones that do show the everyday concerns they expressed: "My Ox is Called Rosella", "The Mother of My Love", "The Angered and

Betrayed Spouse", "The Weaver", "Come Down from the Mountain", "I Stuck a Thorn in my Heart", and "She Was Crying".

Accompanying these songs were the early musicians of the Comino Valley who played the zampogna, the piffero, the organetto and the tamburello. The "zampogna" is the most important of all of these instruments because it came to define the people of Picinisco thoughout Europe. The zampogna is a bagpipe: the bag is made of sheep or goat skin that is cured on the inside (animal hair stays on the outside) and four pipes, bound together as a single stock, are inserted into the bag. The musician blows into an additional pipe to inflate the bag and uses his arms to pump the bag and his fingers to open or close holes in the four pipes. The sound, while much like the bagpipes of Scotland, seems a bit softer and more melodic.

The zampogna was the instrument of choice for shepherds in the mountains because it could be easily transported. Its popularity

spread with these shepherds as they travelled extensively during the transumanza. In the capital city of Naples, during Christmas, zampogna players from Picinisco were hired to play at various events. The zampogna eventually became celebrated throughout the capitals of Europe as many Piciniscani emigrants used it to make their living as street musicians. The beautiful melodies and the colorful appearance of the musicians attracted the attention of artists who immortalized the players in important works of art in every capital during the nineteenth century. Some players became professional musicians in and around Picinisco, playing for weddings and holidays. The zampogna ultimately came to be the principal accompaniment to any musical expression in Picinisco. The "piffero" (also known as a "ciaramella") is a reed instrument much like an oboe. Like the zampogna, the piffero was easy to carry and made the perfect accompaniment to the zampogna. The "organetto" is an accordion, also often made in a very small size for easy transportation. The tamburello is a tambourine.

Dancing to the music of these classic instruments helped to illustrate the story of the lyrics. Specific dances were developed for songs around the holidays or to celebrate the harvest. Long ago, dancing was principally an all-male or all-female activity because society frowned upon any interaction between the sexes. Much later, married men and women were permitted to dance in public, but any unmarried person could not touch the hand of the opposite sex and had to dance with a handkerchief held between them.

Perhaps the most popular dance in the Comino Valley is the "ballarella" (also known as the "saltarello" and thought to be related to the more popular "tarantella"). It is a dance of courtship that allows the audience to appreciate the physical prowess of the dancers. A group of dancers come together in a circle and join arms, holding on to one another at the shoulder, and they move around the circle. North of the Comino Valley, closer to Rome, the dancers skip or leap using athletic gyrations that become increasingly vivacious and it is a fast and lively dance. In the Comino Valley, it is a slightly softer rhythm and less frenetic dance. Today it is performed in Picinisco by couples as well as in groups. La pizzica, another dance of the region, is also part of the family of tarantella dances, but this one involves a couple (male and female or same sex) who wrap their arms around one another to perform the dance.

Another popular local dance is the danza dei nastri (ribbon dance). This is a very technically precise dance where participants using long ribbons strung from a pole and move around the pole so that their ribbons ultimately create a star. (It is very much like a maypole dance). The danza delle mazze (dance of the grain threshing) is a dance for harvest time. Each dancer uses a long stick that simulates the threshing of wheat as they whirl around. The tammurriata is another traditional dance that began as a song accompanied by a drum that looks like a giant tambourine and called a "tammorra." The dance involves a couple who use castanets and wild movements of their arms, representing their daily activities like threshing grain or making pasta, that culminate in expressions of love and devotion. These same dances are still popular and performed regularly in Picinisco during festivities in August.

Chapter 20

Emigration

Most people from Picinisco were born, lived and died there and never ventured farther from home than the market in Atina. However, during the late 1700s and particularly in the 1800s, conditions in Picinisco changed and emigration - first seasonal, then temporary, and eventually permanent - became a necessity for many. There were a variety of factors that led to this mass emigration. The Napoleonic government in Naples had promised peasants that the end of feudalism would give them a chance to own their own land, but that promise never really materialized. The local population continued to grow and farmland was being overworked to keep up with demand. Political upheaval during the end of the Kingdom of Naples gave rise to violence in and around Picinisco as Italy unified and the south rebelled. Following Italian unification, widespread unemployment plagued southern Italy. Improvements in agricultural production in the north of Italy caused food prices all over the country to drop. Large southern landowners invested in equipment that allowed for less labor-intensive and more profitable farming methods. The Italian state instituted universal health care, resulting in further over-population. The new unified government recognized that living conditions in the south of Italy were deplorable but did not have the political will to make a significant investment there. They saw emigration as the answer to the problem; cash being brought back to southern communities by temporary emigrants allowed southerners to begin to buy more land and improve their living conditions, without governmental expense. In the 1880s, as much as 5,000 British pounds per year were being sent home by Piciniscani emigrants. So, as the 1800s were coming to a close, the new government supported and encouraged emigration.

Against this backdrop, it is not surprising that many from Picinisco left to find work elsewhere. The concept of seasonal migration was already a long established practice in Picinisco, as part of the shepherds' regular movements of their flocks, so it was not unusual for the Piciniscani to contemplate leaving home for several months for work. This practice likely began in the late 1700s, though statistics about travel during that time are virtually nonexistent. Beginning in the early 1800s, the first waves of seasonal emigrants went to nearby areas (outside the cities of Naples and Rome) to work as day laborers in the fields. They were able to walk there and back in times when they were not needed on their own farms. The temporary emigration that followed this first wave went further afield - Paris, London, Berlin or Moscow - and many left for several years at a time. People from Picinisco worked abroad as models for artists, sold roasted chestnuts and figurines, and sharpened knives. In Rome, the Piciniscani emigrants played religious hymns on the zampogna and pipes on the streets. Unwilling to accept payment when it was a religious hymn being performed, they insisted on giving the audience members a small carved wooden spoon in exchange for cash gratuities. Other Piciniscani worked the streets of Europe's capitals with trained bears, purportedly captured in the mountains above Picinisco. These earliest temporary migrants returned home to Picinisco bringing with them crucial information about the opportunities for improvement in the world outside Picinisco.

The desperation of the peasant population in Picinisco and the temptation of money available in foreign capitals resulted in impossible choices for families. Many men left their wives and families alone to fend for themselves and went away, sometimes for years, to seek work. Others left with their young families and walked miles each day, through countries where they did not speak the language, having to find food and shelter and any kind of work they could to support themselves on their journey. Parents were lured into virtually selling their children into slavery in some cases. In Picinisco, a local "padrone" would offer to take a child under his care for some period of time in exchange for a payment to the parents, and then use the children as beggars on the streets of large cities like Moscow, Paris and London. The padrone grew rich off the earnings of these poor children. Exploited and often abused, these children were frequently, eventually abandoned by the padrone and left to fend for themselves in a foreign country. It is reported that less than 30% of them ever returned home to Italy.

According to the Italian government, 14 million people left Italy during the period from 1876 through 1914. These statistics are not, however, completely reliable. They are based only on the number of passports issued to Italian citizens, and it is not certain that everyone who got a passport actually left Italy, or that everyone who left Italy did so with a passport. Approximately 44% of these 14 million Italians emigrated to European countries (primarily Austria-Hungary, France, Germany and Switzerland), 30% went to the United States, and 24% went to South American (primarily Argentina and Brazil). The Italian government also estimated that as many as 50% of these emigrants eventually returned home to Italy, though again these statistics are somewhat doubtful. We have slightly more reliable information about Piciniscani emigrants from some of the foreign countries to which they emigrated. From 1870 to 1920, roughly one-third of emigrants from the town of Picinisco went to France, one-third went to England and the remaining third went to Ireland, Germany, Sweden, Denmark, Russia and Scotland. Much of this population movement was in the form of "chain migration," meaning a single individual or family would establish themselves with a business and then send for their wives and children and their cousins and neighbors to help with the new business.

In Great Britain, the Piciniscani helped to establish a whole new industry: ice cream. With the proximity of snow and ice from Mount Meta and the abundance of fruits in the region, the people of Picinisco had all the raw materials at hand to learn to make sorbets and ice cream. The first Italian ice cream peddlers in Great Britain arrived in the 1850s. They brought their recipes with them, making ice cream at home and wandering the streets with their carts yelling "ecco un poco" (have a little). The British people thought they heard them saying "hokey pokey" and the characterization of the Italian ice cream street vendor was born. The Piciniscani came to dominate all aspects of the British ice cream industry, from production of ice cream and cone wafers to refrigeration and transport. Some of the more successful entrepreneurs in Britain were the Picinisco families of the DeMarcos, the Marcantonios, the Arcaris, the Mancinis, the Capaldis, the Pelosis, the Antonellis, and the Crollas. As they grew more successful, these Picinisco families were able to open ice cream cafes that offered an alternative to the pub as a gathering place. Many of Britain's first fish-and-chip shops were also established by Piciniscani emigrants who saw the economic advantages of fast food in Britain. Other emigrants opened confectionary shops, restaurants and entered the catering trades. Still other Piciniscani established themselves as masters in the trades of tiling and stone masonry, hairdressing and importing wines and foodstuffs from Italy.

Italians in Scotland represent an unusual group in migratory history - the vast majority of them are part of a chain migration from two small towns in Italy: Barga and Picinisco. In 1871, the Italian-born population of Scotland was 119; by 1891 it was 1,025 and by 1921 it was 5,654. The Scots embraced these Italian immigrants (unlike Irish immigrants to Scotland) because they created new industries that did not take employment from native Scots. These italo-scots regularly returned to their hometowns to find brides and buy land and build new homes. Many Picinisco emigrants believed that life in Picinisco was much healthier than industrial Scotland, and chose to retire in Picinisco. Still today one can hear a Scottish-accented English spoken in the piazza of Picinisco quite regularly. And cemeteries in Scotland are filled with headstones listing "Picinisco" as the place of birth.

The return of emigrants from all over the world was a regular occurrence and as a result, the Piciniscani knew well what kind of a life they might find elsewhere. Over the years many more left Picinisco to try their luck in a new location. From 1921 through the 1940s, Picinisco's population decreased by almost 1000 people. In the 1950s alone another 500 people left the town. Interestingly, most of those who left kept the traditions of their homeland alive and even today, all over the world, there are groups from Picinisco and the Comino Valley still celebrating their heritage.

Chapter 21

Modeling

Many historical references to the people of Picinisco talk about their attractive physical features. Although small in stature, the Piciniscani were a strong and robust people. Dressed in their traditional brightly-colored costumes and sandals, they were an unusual sight on the streets of the European capitals where they sought work in the 1800s. They were particularly sought after by the artists' community interested in depicting peasant life in southern Italy. Italian peasants from the Comino Valley posed for all the great artists of the period including Corot, Degas, Rodin, Van Gogh, Cezanne, Gauguin, Picasso, Matisse, Renoir, Manet, Sargent, and Whistler, among others.

Artists first became acquainted with the people of the Comino Valley as potential models on the streets of Rome. These temporary migrants attracted attention as a very young, lively group, singing and dancing as they worked the crowds. Artists coming from around the world to study in Rome were always in search of new and intriguing subjects and the "model district" of Rome was born where the artists and the young Ciociaria people found one another, on the Spanish Steps. The models from Picinisco were admired, not just for their classical facial features, but for their muscular and voluptuous bodies, tanned and etched by the forces of their natural habitat, their luxuriant black eyes, and their thick and curly dark hair and bristling beards. For the artists, it was easy to hire models wearing their own unique traditional clothing, with the accessories of their trade (like musical instruments) in hand. These young men and women of Picinisco were used to hard work, and modeling was particularly grueling - long hours maintaining a pose, often requiring the model to carry heavy objects, sometimes on their heads, or to play an instrument - whatever the artist wanted.

People looking for work as a model typically arrived in the city in late fall, after the harvest, and stayed until spring. (In summer, the city heat caused the artists to leave the metropolitan areas and the models returned home to help in the fields). They lived in the poorest of conditions in the city, but the money they could make was crucial to earning a dowry or being able to help their families purchase land. Word quickly spread back in Picinisco about the money that could be made as a model and with each season, many more young people would join this temporary march to Rome and Paris and eventually London. Even the hunt for the best models was a profession: the Ecole des Beaux Artes in Paris hired Nicola Rossi from Picinisco to secure Ciociaria models for its students, and he did quite well with his commissions.

During the 1800s in Rome, male and female models posed at various art schools, but only the men posed in the nude. Most models from the Comino Valley worked for individual artists in their studios, many of which were located in Via Margutta just off the Spanish Steps. Some young women, particularly those living on their own away from their parents and possibly a stricter moral code, did agree to model nude for individual artists and many were taken advantage of in these circumstances. Later, as families began to accompany young people to Rome, a mother or aunt would insist on being present during the session to protect their young girls from unscrupulous artists. In Paris, nude models were not allowed at the Ecole des Beaux Artes, but they were beginning to be used in some of the smaller art schools. Fillipo Colarossi, himself a model from Picinisco, bought an art school in Montparnasse and called it the "Académie Colarossi." Colarossi used male and female nude models from Ciociaria. Colarossi's school was also the first to admit women artists and permit them to draw from nude models.

Among the more well-known Piciniscani models are: Filippo Rossi, Rosalina Tobia and her husband Giovanni Tobia, Domenico Mancini and his brothers Giuseppe and Geremia and his sister-in-law Addolorata Mancini, Orazio Cervi, Gaetano Valvona, Angelo Colarossi (Filippo's brother), Maria Mancini, Addolorata Margiotta, and Alessandro Di Marco. Rosalina Tobia, born in Picinisco in the 1860s, modeled as a young girl in Paris for artists like Modigliani and Whistler. When she finished modeling at age 45, she opened a cafe called "Chez Rosalie" in Montparnasse that became a gathering point for great artists and writers for years. She eventually retired to the south of France and died there in the 1930s. Domenico Mancini and his family settled in the Hammersmith area of London after emigrating from Picinisco and were soon discovered on the streets by the artist Sir William Blake Richmond. He modeled throughout his life for artists and sculptors in London. The Mancini brothers were known for having worked to improve the conditions of models in London and helping to found the first models' trade union at the Royal Academy schools. Orazio Cervi went to London where he modeled for the sculptor Sir William Hamo Thornycroft. Through his connection with Thornycroft he was introduced to the author D. H. Lawrence, whom Cervi hosted in his home in Picinisco in 1919. It was this visit that caused Lawrence to write about Picinisco in his novel "The Lost Girl". In 2001, an unpublished autobiography by Gaetano Valvona was discovered by members of his family. Valvona worked as a model in Paris and later in London in the late 1800s and had a particularly close relationship with the sculptor Lord Leighton.

Chapter 22

Famous Piciniscani

There are several Piciniscani (or descendants of Piciniscani) who are known well to the world outside of Picinisco:

Angelo Vincenzo Franchini. Probably the first person born in Picinisco to have international acclaim is Franchini, also known as Vincent "Il Franquin" or "Francquein" de Saint Ange. He was born in Picinisco and moved to Paris around 1617. He was famous as a fencing teacher to King Louis XIV of France. The king made him a maestro in 1652 and gave him a noble title in 1669. He died in Paris in 1670.

Ernesto Capocci. Capocci was born in Picinisco in 1798. He was a renowned mathematician and astronomer, ultimately becoming the Director of the Astronomical Observatory of Capodimonte. He was well known in the scientific circles of Europe, receiving awards for his work in Berlin, Paris and London. He wrote many articles about astronomy and later in life he became an author. His novel, printed in 1838, was entitled "The First Viceroy of Naples". In 1848 he became a Senator in the first Italian Parliament. He died in 1864. The main piazza in Picinisco is named after Ernesto Capocci.

Antonio de Antiquis. Born in Picinisco in 1827, de Antiquis studied under the first public school teacher of Picinisco, Lorenzo Boni. He continued his studies at the seminary in Sora and later in Naples. In 1860, he fought with Garibaldi in Naples. He became a highly respected professor and author of a textbook used throughout Italy, as well as many poems admired in literary circles. He died in Picinisco in 1912.

Filippo Colarossi. Colarossi was born in Picinisco in 1841. As a young person, he moved to Paris (around 1855) where he and his brother became models for artists. In 1870, Colarossi bought an art school in Paris which he later renamed "Académie Colarossi" The studio became an important alternative to the Ecole des Beaux Arte for many students, particularly for women artists who were not allowed at the Ecole. Colarossi was unique in his use of male and female nude models in his studio. Among his students were John Singer Sargent, Gauguin and Modigliani. Colarossi was also a painter and a sculptor. He died in 1930.

Angelo Colarossi. Angelo Colarossi, brother of Filippo, was born in 1838 in Picinisco and went with his brother to Paris where they both modeled. He later emigrated to London where his son, Angelo Colarossi Jr., was born in 1875. Father and son modeled in London for some of the great artists. The son modeled for sculptor Alfred Gilbert's famous statue "Anteros" on the Shaftsbury Memorial Fountain in Piccadilly Circus in London. Angelo Sr. died in 1916 and his son in 1949.

Giustino Ferri. Ferri was born in Picinisco in 1856. He graduated from law school in Naples and then went to Rome, where he worked as a prominent journalist and eventually became a prolific author. He wrote 15 novels, the most widely acclaimed being La Camminante, published in 1908. He died in 1913.

Leonardo Domenico Pelosi. Don Pelosi was born in Picinisco in the 1900s. He moved to London and had a family and became a songwriter. In the 1930s, he wrote many popular English songs like "Kiss Me Goodnight Sergeant Major," "Till the Poppies Bloom Again," and "The Stars Will Remember," which was recorded by Frank Sinatra.

Dionigi Antonelli, Monsignor Antonelli was born in Picinisco in 1925. He studied at the seminary in Sora and was ordained in 1950. After earning several university degrees, and spending years as a teacher and professor, he began writing about the Comino Valley. His first work was about the Madanna di Canneto, published in the 1960s. Since then he has written many scholarly treatises and is a renowned lecturer who lives in Picinisco.

Roberto Luigi Valente. Valente is a painter, born in Picinisco in 1926. His works can be found in Rome and London and New York.

Peter Capaldi. A British actor, famous for his portrayal of "Dr. Who" in the long-running television show of the same name, is the grandson of Giovanni Battista Capaldi, born in Picinisco in 1885.

D. H. Lawrence and Orazio Cervi. The famed American author and his wife stayed in the home of Picinisco resident Orazio Cervi, a model for artists in London, for several weeks as guests in 1919. He later wrote a book, called "The Lost Girl," part of which takes place in a mountain-top village widely acknowledged to be based on the town of Picinisco.

Mary Contini. Contini has written two novels; "Dear Francesca" and "Dear Olivia", both of which deal with her Picinisco family and their journey to the United Kingdom. Mary was born in Scotland and is part owner of the famous Edinburgh delicatessen Valvona & Crolla in Edinburgh.

Anita Arcari. Anita is an author who recently published a book about her Picinisco family called The Hokey Pokey Man. This book tells the story of a young man who leaves Picinisco and makes a life in England in the ice cream business. Anita is a lecturer in Computing in Wales.

Maria Corelli. Maria Corelli wrote a book entitled "In Love and War: A Letter to my Parents." Although born in Great Britain, Corelli moved to Picinisco as a young woman and describes her time there during World War II.

Teresa Arcari Capocci. Capocci was born in Scotland in 1914 and wrote about her emigration to Picinisco, where she stayed in the hamlet of Serre during World War II, in her book entitled "Alle Serre di Picinisco".

Chapter 23

Holidays

The calendar year of holidays celebrated in Picinisco is (and was historically) primarily based upon religious celebrations.

January 5th - The Night Before Epiphany. Much like Santa Claus, the "Befana" (an elderly woman who flies on a broom) visits the homes of the town through the chimney and leaves toys, biscuits and candies in the stockings of "good" children and ash and coal in the stockings of "bad" children. There is also a candlelight vigil held in town.

January 17th - St. Antonio Feast Day. Saint Antonio is the patron saint of animals and on this day there is a public ceremony for blessing the animals of the town. Years ago, families washed and decorated their animals and brought one of each type to the blessing. A large celebration was held in the piazza in town and all those from the surrounding villages participated and a mass followed.

February 2nd - Candlemas. This is the feast of the purification of the Virgin Mary and the blessing of the candles used in the Church for the coming year. Blessing the candles protects against lightening and hail. This day is also a celebration of the halfway point between winter solstice and the spring equinox.

February 3rd - St Blaise Feast Day. Saint Blaise is the patron saint of sore throats and this day a cotton cloth is dipped in oil blessed by the priest and applied to the neck to protect against throat problems.

February - Carnival. This is a celebration that begins with the Epiphany and lasts until Lent when the faithful will give up something they value during the 40 days beginning on Ash Wednesday. In the Comino Valley it begins with Giovedi Grasso (fat Thursday) when people gather together and eat at least seven times. Carnival is celebrated with festivals and parades generally taking place on Shrove Tuesday.

March 18th - St. Joseph's Bonfire. This day is a combined celebration of the life of Joseph and of the end of winter and beginning of Spring in the Comino Valley. The bonfire is the burning of the winter and an alignment of man with the forces of nature. People sing, dance and eat around the bonfires.

March 19th - Father's Day. This celebration of fathers goes hand in hand with the celebration of Saint Joseph.

Palm Sunday - Boys carry a large olive branch to each house in the village and "sing the palms." At the end of their song they are invited into the houses for food and drinks. In the evening there is a procession depicting the Stations of the Cross, ending in the reenactment of the crucification in front of the castle.

Easter Sunday - Mass is followed by a large family lunch.

Easter Monday - Pasquetta. In the Comino Valley, this is a day off of work and usually a day of family get-togethers and picnics.

May 1st - Labor Day. This is a holiday to honor workers.

May 8th - Feast of San Michele. A bonfire is made in honor of the Saint and a tasting is laid out of various products from the region.

June (60 days after Easter) - Feast of Corpus Christi. On this day the people in the Comino Valley celebrate with an "infiorata" - images of daily life or religious scenes are depicted in flowers laid on the ground in the village squares.

June (first weekend) - Feast of the Orapi. A festival celebrating wild spinach.

June 23rd evening - Eve of the Feast of St. John the Baptist. Bonfires are lit in the towns of the Comino Valley on St. John's eve to protect people from disease and to cast out devils and witches. This is the night that people gather walnuts to make "nocino" a famous walnut liqueur.

June 24th - Feast of St. John the Baptist and Summer Solstice. Villagers share gifts of flowers and small presents to become the "friends of St. John".

July 26th - St. Anne's Feast Day. Saint Anne, mother of the Virgin Mary, is celebrated this day with pilgrimages to Vallepietra to the Shrine of the Holy Trinity. This is located in a rocky area where a natural cut into the mountains exists. Pilgrims touch the rock with their hands on the way into the sanctuary and then walk out of the sanctuary backwards in respect for the Holy Trinity.

August 9 - 10 - Festival of the Sheep. This celebration of sheep and shepherds in Picinisco includes demonstrations of cheese and wine-making and milking, lectures on history, ethnic music, food markets, etc. It is known throughout Italy and probably the largest celebration of the year.

August 10th - Feast of San Lorenzo. This is a celebration of the feast day of the patron saint of Picinisco - Saint Lorenzo. The statue of San Lorenzo is carried in a procession through town and afterwards there are celebrations everywhere with music and dancing.

August 15th - Ferragosto. A public holiday when most Italians begin their summer vacation. Trips to the beach, lake or mountain are typical on this day.

August 18th - 22nd - Pilgrimage to the Sanctuary of the Madonna of Canneto/Historical Parade in Picinisco/Celebrations of Picinisco Emigrants and Feast of Saint Maria Assunta. The Sanctuary of the Madonna is thought to have existed as early as the third or fourth century as a pagan place of worship. It is located in the valley of Canneto - high up among the beech trees in the foothills of Mount Meta. The festival begins on August 18th when a reproduction of the statue is carried from Settefrati (a neighboring town) and remains at Canneto until August 22nd. Different towns in the region (including Picinisco) participate by sending their own pilgrims walking to the Sanctuary behind their local banners. On August 21st, there is a large procession from the Sanctuary to the head of the River Melfa and from there the procession continues back to Settefrati on August 22nd. In Picinisco, August 18th and 19th are given to historical parades in costume and music. August 19th is the feast in honor of the emigrant Piciniscani all over the world. On August 20th and 21st the Piciniscani celebrate the Feast of Maria Assunta - the patron saint of the Church of Santa Maria Assunta.

September (3rd Sunday) - Celebration of mushrooms.

November 1st - All Saints Day. This is a public holiday. The people of Picinisco leave candles lit outside their front doors and on their tables are water, wine, glasses and boiled chestnuts to honor the dead.

December 8th - Feast of the Immaculate Conception.

November 11th - St. Martin's Day. Saint Martin is the patron saint of winemakers. On this holiday the new season's wine is ready for tasting and in the Comino Valley they serve it with roasted chestnuts.

December 13th - St. Lucia's Day. St. Lucia's Day is at the winter solstice during Advent and is celebrated as the festival of lights. This is the beginning of the pre-Christmas music of the zampogna and the ciaramella.

December 24th - Christmas Eve. A special dinner of fish is prepared. Midnight mass takes place in Picinisco at the Church of San Lorenzo. During the "Presente Vivante" the townspeople reenact the birth of Christ with costumed shepherds, three kings, and the Holy Family.

December 31st - New Year's Eve. Tradition calls for eating a plate of lentils (which resemble ancient coins) to insure the next year is a financially prosperous one. Also people wear red for good luck. Families play a game called "tombola" which is like bingo.

Chapter 24

Picinisco Today

Today Picinisco is a tourist's paradise with things to offer the historian, the foodie, the naturalist and the sports enthusiast.

It is easy to imagine what it was like in Picinisco hundreds of years ago as its medieval beginnings are well preserved in the town center. The original town gates can be seen between the remains of the original walls of the eleventh century. The fourteenth century Church of San Lorenzo and bell tower sits in the center, with beautiful stone houses that have been lovingly restored surrounding it. Everywhere there are iron balconies, stone-paved streets and pretty entryways throughout the town. The doors of all the homes are particularly beautiful with their large curved archways, often decorated with stone, and many painted colors.

You can wander through the castle grounds and see the eleventh-century tower that symbolizes the town of Picinisco. Montano Park offers a beautiful walkway from the castle gate to a charming war memorial overlooking the picturesque mountains behind Picinisco. But perhaps the most gorgeous view from Picinisco is found in the Piazza Capocci, where one can easily spend a perfect evening with a bottle of wine and some companions, watching the sun set over the Comino Valley.

Picinisco has a small museum dedicated to the lives of the Piciniscani farmers and shepherds. The Church of San Lorenzo holds records for the births, marriages and deaths of the Piciniscani, beginning in the late 1500s, a treasure trove for genealogists. According to scholars familiar with this region, it is very unusual to find early church records such as these; many were lost over time and many more were destroyed during World War II. Casa Lawrence, a lovely bed and breakfast, also offers another glimpse into Picinisco's past. In 1919 D.H. Lawrence and his wife Freida stayed in the main house there for several weeks and D.H. Lawrence's book "The Lost Girl" includes passages about a mountaintop town based on Picinisco. The main house has been refurbished in the manner it existed during Lawrence's stay there. There is also a library with works of D.H. Lawrence, as well as books about the Comino Valley.

You can take a lovely drive up the mountain to visit the Sanctuary of the Madonna di Canneto. The road leads through a pre-historic forest, dark and damp, to a clearing where you find the main church of the Madonna. Further up the road you can explore the Melfa River and the tracks leading up into the mountains. The entire National Park of Abruzzo, Lazio and Molise is available for all kinds of sport. Here you can hike the old tratturi (paths) that shepherds used for hundreds of years; there are many challenging routes for mountain biking in the Park; or you can go for a horseback ride or challenge yourself to serious rock climbing. Best of all, the park preserves the natural flora as well as the animal life of the region, particularly the Apennine wolf, the golden eagle and the brown bear. Within the borders of the Park there are many beautiful historic towns, like Pescasseroli and Opi, to visit. Park Avventura (Adventure Park) offers hiking, zip-lining and education about the natural environment for all ages. Up at Prati di Mezzo, there is skiing in the winter, both downhill and cross-country, hiking in the summer, camping, picnicking, and mountain biking, at this beautiful location inside the National Park of Abruzzo, Lazio and Molise.

For the foodie, there are many opportunities to indulge. There are several restaurants in Picinisco serving local cuisine: La Locanda di Arturo sits just below the piazza and offers a menu full of delicious local dishes, Casa Lawrence offers a restaurant featuring local foods and the lovely La Caciosteria for cheese, salami and wine of the region, as well as Bellavista Pizza, for its bar and excellent pizza. The most prized local commodities are: olive oil, cheese, meat (pig, sheep and goat), salami, mushrooms and truffles, and the local wine. The most famous of these products produced today

is pecorino cheese. Pecorino cheese from Picinisco has received the coveted DOP rating identifying it as an artisanal cheese. It is made from the milk of sheep that graze on the fertile mountainous slopes of Picinisco. Their consumption of the herbs growing wild in the region gives the pecorino its rich and coveted taste.

Ricotta is a whey cheese made from the sheep or goats milk whey left over from the production of pecorino cheese. Again, the fact that the animals in the region are feeding on the rich mountain pastures above Picinisco makes this cheese unique. It is best when eaten just after it is made; creamy, rich and distinctive in flavor. It often served with freshly baked bread and some honey. Marzolina cheese is an ancient cheese recently revived by the cheese makers of Picinisco. It is made with the milk of goats' first lactation after giving birth, generally in March (hence its name - marzo means March). Salsiccia della Valcomino is a special sausage made of the organ meats and fat of pigs fed on chestnuts and acorns. It is seasoned with chili, pepper, orange peel and garlic, and often diced apples. Some of the popular recipes from Picinisco include: "pasta con gli orapi" which is made with the wide fettuccine noodle served with wild spinach. "Abb'ticchie" is a dish made of lamb entrails stuffed with celery and seasoned and baked in the oven. "Calascioni" is a puffed pastry, shaped like a round ravioli, that is stuffed with egg and pecorino cheese baked in the oven. "Calascinetti" is a "panzotti" (circular folded pastry) filled with a chestnut paste.

After dinner, all Italians love a "digestivo" - a liqueur designed to help with digestion. In every part of Italy, the local, homemade variety is a prized treat. In Picinisco, it is "Genziana," made from the roots of the wild gentian plant or "Nocino" a liqueur made from walnuts. Also from the region is "Ratafia" made from cherries, red wine and flavored with nutmeg and cinnamon.

Many people are attracted to Picinisco to join the hunt for some of the wild local delicacies. The mountain asparagus which is very small, thin and slightly bitter is a big attraction. Others come to hunt for black truffles. It is often difficult for outsiders to find these truffles as traditional foraging areas are handed down from father to son and closely guarded.

Recently the di Ciacca family, headed by Cesidio di Ciacca, founded the "I Ciacca Società Agricola", with the goal of resurrecting traditional Picinisco farming methods and products. The group has already planted vines and sought DOC recognition for the almost-extinct variety "Maturano" and will be opening a winery soon. They grow olives and produce a unique extra-virgin olive oil for sale, as well as honey, and jams and preserves. All the products come from family farmland, in the tradition of years gone by. The Society is presently working on a new venture called, the "I Ciacca Foundation for Food Excellence." It is a collaboration between educational institutions in Scotland and Italy, and will provide young people with an opportunity study and work in agriculture, gastronomy, and hospitality.

August is still the preferred time of year to visit Picinisco for the "Pastorizia in Festival" the annual celebration of the shepherds of Picinisco that has food, wine, music and dancing as well as a celebration of the arts and crafts of the region. There are demonstrations of cheese-making, guided walking tours with shepherds and their flocks, and educational talks about the biodiversity of the region and the age-old transumanza. Every evening there is traditional music and dancing. Immediately following this festival is the celebration of San Lorenzo, the patron saint of the town of Picinisco. There is a parade through the town and special foods and more music and dancing. A couple of days later, after Ferragosto, is the pilgrimage to Canneto when literally thousands of people walk from Picinisco to the church in Canneto. Over the following days, there are celebrations of the Piciniscani emigrants and the patron saint of the Church of Santa Maria Assunta. Parades wind through the town with participants in historic costumes and musicians playing historic instruments.

Today there are several choices of places to stay in Picinisco. Sotto le Stelle offers lavish apartments with gorgeous terraces right in the heart of town. Chez Nous is a lovely bed and breakfast located just outside the town walls. Casa Lawrence also offers a comfortable bed and breakfast in the nearby locale of Serre. There are holiday apartments available for rent in the area as well.

The entire Comino Valley awaits exploration. The Abbey at Montecassino is a historic gem. The towns of Settefrati, San Donato Valcomino and Alvito. The lake at Posta Fibreno. A vacation of several weeks would be required to partake in all that the area offers.

Websites

www.comune.picinisco.fr.it
www.picinisco.net
www.picinisco.com
livepicinisco.com
www.prolocopicinisco.it
www.valdicomino.it
www.valledicomino.it
www.parcoabruzzo.it
www.ciociariaturismo.it
www.abbaziamontecassino.org
www.madonnadicanneto.it
www.indianaparkpicinisco.it
www.lalocandadiarturo.it
www.casalawrence.it
www.pasoriziainfestival.it
www.sottolestellepicinisco.it
www.bbcheznous.it
www.iciaccapicinisco.com

Bibliography

Books & Periodicals - English

Appel, Will. The Evil Eye and Peasant Identity in Southern Italy. (PhD Dissertation). New York: Cornell University, 1975

Antinoro-Pollozzi, J. Southern Italian Society: Its Peasantry and Change. Massachusetts: Alpine Press, 1968.

Arcari, Anita. The Hokey Pokey Man. U.K.: Y Lolfa, 2010.

Astarita, Tommaso. Between Salt Water and Holy Water – A History of Southern Italy. New York: W.W. Norton & Co., 2005.

Astarita, Tommaso. The Continuity of Feudal Power: The Caracciolo di Brienza in Spanish Naples. Cambridge; New York: Cambridge University Press, 1992.

Audry, Suzzane. Multiculturalism in Practice – Irish, Jewish, Italian and Pakistani Migration to Scotland. Vermont: Ashgate Publishing Company, 2000.

Barca, Stefania. Enclosing Water: Nature and Political Economy in a Mediterranean Valley 1796 - 1916. Cambridge: White Horse Press, 2010.

Bell, Rudolph. Fate and Honor, Family and Village: Demographic and Cultural Change in Rural Italy Since 1800. Chicago: University of Chicago Press, 1979.

Black, Christopher F. Early Modern Italy: A Social History. London; New York: Routledge, 2001.

Bloch, Herbert. Montecassino in the Middle Ages. Massachusetts: Harvard University Press, 1986.

Brown, Virginia. Terra Sancti Benedicti: Studies in the Paleography, History and Liturgy of Medieval Southern Italy. Rome, 2005.

Canziani, Estella. Through the Apennines and the Lands of the Abruzzi Landscape and Peasant Life. Boston: Houghton Mifflin Company, 1928.

Canziani, Estella. "Abruzzese Folklore" Folk-Lore Vol. 39, No. 3 (Sept, 1928).

Carlyle, Margaret. The Awakening of Southern Italy. London; New York: Oxford University Press, 1962.

Castiglione, Caroline. Patrons and Adversaries: Nobles and Villagers in Italian Politics, 1640-1760. New York: Oxford University Press, 2005.

Colpi, Terri. Italians Forward: A Visual History of the Italian American Community in Great Britain. Edinburgh: Mainstream Publishing, 1991.

Colpi, Terri. The Italian Factor: The Italian Community in Great Britain. Edinburgh: Mainstream Publishing, 1991.

Contini, Mary. Dear Francesca – A Cookbook With Love. London: Ebury Press, 2002.

Contini, Mary. Dear Olivia: An Italian Journey of Love and Courage. Edinburgh: Cannongate Press, 2006.

Corelli, Maria. In Love and War: A Letter to my Parents. London: Short Books, 2001.

Cornelisen, Ann. Torregreca: Life, Death, and Miracles in a Southern Italian Town. Boston: Little, Brown, 1969.

Cornelisen, Ann. Women of the Shadows: Wives and Mothers of Southern Italy. Boston: Little, Brown, 1976.

d'Agostino, Eugenio (aka Cagliardo Coraggioso) The Wandering Minstrel. London: Oxford University Press, 1938.

Di Scala, Spencer. Italy From Revolution to Republic. Colorado: Westview Press, 1995.

Douglass, William. Emigration in a South Italian Town: An Anthropological History. New Jersey: Rutgers University Press, 1984.

Finley, Milton. The Most Monstrous of Wars: The Napoleonic Guerrilla War in Southern Italy, 1806-1811. South Carolina: The University of South Carolina Press, 1994.

Fortier, Anne-Marie. Migrant Belongings: Memory, Space, Identity. Oxford; New York: Berg, 2000.

Gregorovius, Ferdinand. Latian Summers and an Excursion in Umbria. London, 1902.

Holmes, George. The Oxford Illustrated History of Italy. Oxford; New York: Oxford University Press, 1997.

Kertzer, David, Saller, Richard. The Family in Italy from Antiquity to the Present. New Haven: Yale University Press, 1991.

Lawrence, D.H. The Lost Girl. London: Martin Secker, 1920.

Levi, Carlo. Christ Stopped at Eboli. New York: Farrar, Straus & Co., 1947.

Loud, G.A. Montecassino and Benevento in the Middle Ages: Essays in South Italian Church History. Great Britain: Aldershot, 2000.

Loud, G.A. The Latin Church in Norman Italy. Leeds: Cambridge University Press, 2008.

MacFarlane, Charles. Popular Customs, Sports and Recollections of the South of Italy. London: Charles Knight & Co., 1846.

Marino, John. Pastoral Economics in the Kingdom of Naples. Baltimore: Johns Hopkins University Press, 1988.

Matthews, Jeff: Taylor, David: Marruccu, Iris. A Brief History of Naples and Other Tales. Naples: Fotopragetti Press, 1994.

Miller, Jay Martin. The Complete Story of the Italian Earthquake Horror. Chicago: NP, 1909.

Morton, H.V. A Traveler in Southern Italy. New York: Dodd, Mead, 1969.

Mowbray, Jay Henry, Ph.D. Italy's Great Horror of Earthquake and Tidal Wave. Pennsylvania: National Publishing Co., 1909.

Newby, Eric. Love and War in the Apennines. U.K.: Hodder & Stoughton, 1971.

Piccioni, Luigi (Translated by Simona Noce & Revised by Cheryl Chapman). Ninety Years of the Abruzzo National Park 1922-2012. Newcastle upon Tyne: Cambridge Scholars Publishing, 2013.

Sakellariou, Eleni. Southern Italy in the Late Middle Ages. Boston: Brill, 2012.

Sarti, Roland. Long Live the Strong: A History of Rural Society in the Apennine Mountains. Amherst: University of Massachusetts Press, 1985.

Schachter, Gustav. Rural Life in Southern Italy. American Journal of Economics & Sociology, 1965.

Sereni, Emilio. Storia del Paesaggio Agrario Italiano. Rome-Bari: Laterza, 1961; translated by R. Burr Litchfield as History of the Italian Agricultural Landscape; New Jersey: Princeton University Press, 1997.

Silverman, Sydel F. "Agricultural Organization, Social Structure, and Values in Italy: Amoral Familism Reconsidered". American Anthropologist, Vol. 70, No. 1, 1968.

Skinner, Patricia. Family Power in Southern Italy: The Duchy of Gaeta and Its Neighbors, 850 - 1139. Cambridge, New York: Cambridge University Press, 1995.

Tullio, Paolo. North of Naples, South of Rome. London: Hamish, Hamilton, 1994.

Wilson, Perry. Gender, Family and Sexuality: The Private Sphere in Italy, 1860 - 1945. London, New York: Palgrave Macmillan, 2004.

Zucchi, John. The Little Slaves of the Harp: Italian Child Street Musicians in Nineteenth Century Paris, London and New York. Montreal: McGill-Queens University Press, 1992.

Books & Periodicals - Italian

Antonelli, Dionigi. L'Antica Chiesa Parrocchiale e Collegiata di S. Maria Assunta di Picinisco. Picinisco: NP, 2013.

Antonelli, Dionigi. Alvito dalle Origini al Sec. XIV. Castelliri: Printhouse, 1999.

Antonelli, Dionigi. Il Santuario di Canneto. Veroli: Tip. dell'Abbazia di Casamari,1969.

Antonelli, Dionigi. Settefrati nel Medioevo di Val Comino. Castelliri: Tipografia editrice Pasquarelli, 1994.

Antonelli, Dionigi. Il Castello Medioevale di Picinisco. Rome: C&V, 1997.

Antonelli, Dionigi. La Chiesa Collegiata di San Lorenzo L. e M. Picinisco: NP, 1993.

Antonelli, Dionigi. Gli Ospedali delle Parrocchie e degli Ordini Religiosi Esistenti nella Città e nella Diocesi di Sora dal Sec. XI al Sec. XIX. Sora: NO, 2009.

Arcari, Vincenzo. Storia Di Picinisco. Rome: Apice, 1959.

Caira, Luciano & Orlandi, Vincenzo. Valle di Comino - appena ieri. Gaeta: Albatros, 2001.

Capocci, Ernesto (pseudonym E. C. di Belmonte). Il Primo Viceré di Napoli. Parigi; Londra, 1838.

Capocci, Teresa Arcari. Alle Serre di Picinisco. Memorie di Emigrazione, Guerra e Liberazione. Centro Studi Sorani Patriarca, 2006.

Castrucci, Paolo Mattia. Descrizione del Ducato d'Alvito nel Regno di Napoli in Campagna. Roma, 1633; reprinted Stamperio Piscopo, 1863 and A. Forni, 1978.

Cedrone, Domenico. Canti e culti della Valle di Comino. Picinisco (FR), Centro Studi Ricerche "Ass. Int. Calamus", 1999.

Cirelli, Filippo. Il Regno Delle Due Sicilie. Napoli, 1853.

Coarelli, Filippo. Abruzzo, Molise. Roma: Laterza, 1984.

Coccia, Stefano; Fiorani, Donatella; Rizzello, Marcello; Giammaria, Gioacchino. Castelli del Lazio Meridionale: Contributi di Storia, Architettura ed Archeologia. Roma: Laterza, 1998.

Colacicchi, Luigi. Canti Popolari di Ciociaria. Attl del III Congresso Nazionale di Arti e Tradizioni Popolari," Roma, 1936.

Comitato per la Attività Culturali dell'Anno Galio. Il Ducato di Alvito nell'Età dei Gallio. Alvito: Banca della Ciociaria, 1997.

DeFelice, Emidio. Dizionario dei Cognomi Italiani. Milan: Arnoldo Modadori, 1978.

Giammaria, Gioacchino. Tradizioni Popolari Musicali nel Lazio Meridionale. Anagni: Instituto di Storia e di Arte Del Lazio Meridionale, 1999.

Giannetti, Floriana. Picinisco e il territorio della Valcomino dalla fine del 1500 all'inizio del 1900. Cassino: Idest, 2012.

Giannetti, Luigi. Pastorizia. Sora: SIAE, 2000.

Iannazzi, Ugo; Beranger, Eugenio Maria; Clemente, Pietro; D'Aureli, Marco; Caruso, Fulvia. Gente di Ciociaria. Arce: XV Comunità Montana Valle di Liri,2007.

Lauri, Achille. Atina Potens e Paesi Vicini. Sora: V. D'Amico, 1914.

Leti Messina, Vittorio. La Val di Comino - Problemi e propositi per una pianificazione intercomunale. Frosinone: Chamber of Commerce and Industry, 1973

Mancini, Armando. La Storia di Atina - Raccolta di Scritti Vari. 2nd Edition. Bologna: Forni, 2012.

Marsilli, Renata. La Valle di Comino - Note Antropologiche. Roma: Istituto di Geografia dell'Universita di Roma, 1965.

Orlandi, Serafino. Cenni Storici di Picinisco. Manuscript, 1831.

Paone, Natalino La Transumanza: Immagini di una Civiltà. Isernia: Iannone Cosmos, 1987.

Pelosi, Mauro. Picinisco. lulu.com, 2012.

Petrocelli, Edilio. La Civita della Transumanza: Storia, Cultura e Valorizzazione dei Tratturi del Mondo Pastorale in Abruzzi, Molise, Puglia, Campania e Basilicata. Isernia: Iannone Cosmos, 1999.

Pistelli, Emilio. I Confini della Terra di San Benedetto. Cassino: NP, 2006.

Policella, Loreto (coordinator). Architettura Rurale della Val Comino. Fornia: Grafica Snc, 2001.

Rizzello, Marcello & Sorrentino, Antonio. Atina dall'alto Medioevo alla Fine dell'età Feudale (Sec. V-XIX). Edizioni Albatros, 1993.

Santoro, Domenico. Pagine Sparse di Storia Alvitana. Chieti, 1908.

Santulli, Michele. Modelle e Modelli Ciociari Nell'Arte Europea a Roma, Parigi, Londra nel 1800 - 1900. Arpino: Edizioni Ciociaria Sconosciuta, 2011.

Silone, Ignazio. Fontamara. Rome, 1933.

Tauleri, Buonaventura. Memorie Istoriche dell'antica Citta d'Atina. Napoli, 1702

Toto, Lorenzo & Patini, Patrizia. Cibo e Territorio, La Ciociaria Eno-gastronomica. Frosinone, 2006.

Trigona, Simon Luca. Atina e il suo Territorio nel Medioevo: Storia e Topografia di una Citta di Frontiera. Montecassino: Pubblicazioni Cassinesi, 2003.

Vittorio, Fabrizio & Scappaticci, Rinaldo. Album di Paese. Sora: Arti Grafiche Pasquarelli, 2003.

Zaccaria Mari; Maria Teresa Petrara; Maria Sperandio; Jean Coste. Il Lazio tra antichità e medioevo: studi in memoria di Jean Coste. Roma: Quasar, 1999.

VIRGINIA ARCARI

Virginia Arcari finished college with a degree in history and promptly put it aside to attend law school and move to New York City, where she practiced for over 20 years in international and business tax planning. Her love of history and an unwillingness to abandon years of research experience inspired Virginia to turn next to a project that had always fascinated her – the origin of her father's Italian-Scottish family. She ultimately published a book for her family that included over 500 years of family history. That family history began in Picinisco, Italy.

The lack of historical material about Picinisco always bothered Virginia. Among her relatives in Scotland, she found others with a "Picinisco connection" who had the same questions about the town's origins. So began her quest to learn the Italian language, spend time in Picinisco, and gather together any and all material that would uncover some of the mysteries of the beautiful mountaintop town in the Comino Valley.

Virginia Arcari still lives in New York City with her husband. For the past ten years, she has spent several months at a time in Italy soaking up the culture and improving her language skills. She and her husband travel extensively, and particularly enjoy spending time with her large Arcari family in Scotland.

21558578R00094

Printed in Great Britain
by Amazon